Favorite Recipes

Publications International, Ltd.

Special thanks to the Campbell's Kitchen and Jane M. Freiman, Group Manager.

Pictured on the front cover: Spinach Ricotta Gnocchi *(page 76)*.

Pictured on the back cover *(top to bottom)*: Classic Tuna Noodle Casserole *(page 42)* and Skillet Chicken & Rice *(page 94)*.

ISBN-13: 978-1-4508-2361-6
ISBN-10: 1-4508-2361-0

Library of Congress Control Number: 2011921873

Manufactured in China.

8 7 6 5 4 3 2 1

Microwave Cooking: Microwave ovens vary in wattage. Use the cooking times as guidelines and check for doneness before adding more time.

Preparation/Cooking Times: Preparation times are based on the approximate amount of time required to assemble the recipe before cooking, baking, chilling or serving. These times include preparation steps such as measuring, chopping and mixing. The fact that some preparations and cooking can be done simultaneously is taken into account. Preparation of optional ingredients and serving suggestions is not included.

contents

Family
Favorites

Classic Beef Stroganoff
(recipe page 6)

Classic Beef Stroganoff

MAKES 4 SERVINGS ■ **PREP TIME:** 20 MINUTES ■ **COOK TIME:** 20 MINUTES

1   boneless beef sirloin steak, ¾-inch thick, cut into 2-inch pieces

    Cracked black pepper

1   tablespoon vegetable oil

1   medium onion, finely chopped (about ½ cup)

1   can (10¾ ounces) Campbell's® Condensed Cream of Mushroom Soup (Regular *or* 98% Fat Free)

½   cup water

¼   cup dry sherry

1   tablespoon tomato paste

¼   cup plain yogurt

    Hot cooked medium egg noodles

    Chopped fresh parsley

1. Season the beef with the black pepper.

2. Heat the oil in a 10-inch skillet over medium-high heat. Add the beef and cook until well browned, stirring often. Remove the beef from the skillet. Pour off any fat.

3. Reduce the heat to medium. Add the onion and cook until tender.

4. Stir in the soup, water, sherry, if desired, and tomato paste and heat to a boil. Return the beef to the skillet and cook until the beef is cooked through. Remove the skillet from the heat. Stir in the yogurt. Serve the beef mixture over the noodles and sprinkle with the parsley.

 Family Favorites

Beefy Fajitas with a Twist

MAKES 4 SERVINGS ▪ **PREP TIME:** 15 MINUTES ▪ **COOK TIME:** 25 MINUTES

- 1 tablespoon vegetable oil
- 1 boneless beef top round steak (about 1 pound), cut into strips
- 1 medium green pepper, cut into 2-inch-long strips (about 1½ cups)
- 1 medium onion, sliced (about ½ cup)
- 1 can (10¼ ounces) Campbell's® Beef Gravy
- 8 flour tortillas (8-inch), warmed
  Shredded Cheddar cheese
  Pace® Chunky Salsa

1. Heat the oil in a 10-inch skillet over medium-high heat. Add the beef and cook until it's well browned, stirring often. Pour off any fat.

2. Add the pepper and onion to the skillet and cook until the vegetables are tender-crisp. Stir in the gravy and cook until the mixture is hot and bubbling.

3. Spoon the beef mixture onto the tortillas. Top with the cheese and salsa. Wrap the tortillas around the filling.

Campbell's 7

Creamy Chicken Enchiladas

MAKES 6 SERVINGS ▪ **PREP TIME:** 20 MINUTES ▪ **BAKE TIME:** 40 MINUTES

- 1 can (10¾ ounces) Campbell's® Condensed Cream of Chicken Soup (Regular *or* 98% Fat Free)
- 1 container (8 ounces) sour cream
- 1 cup Pace® Picante Sauce
- 2 teaspoons chili powder
- 2 cups chopped cooked chicken
- 1 cup shredded Monterey Jack cheese (4 ounces)
- 12 flour tortillas (8-inch), warmed
- 1 medium tomato, chopped (about 1 cup)
- 1 green onion, sliced (about 2 tablespoons)

1. Mix the soup, sour cream, picante sauce and chili powder in a small bowl.

2. Stir **1 cup** of the soup mixture, chicken and cheese in a medium bowl.

3. Spoon about ¼ **cup** of the chicken mixture down the center of each tortilla. Roll up the tortillas and place them seam-side down in 13×9-inch (3-quart) shallow baking dish. Pour the remaining soup mixture over the filled tortillas. **Cover**.

4. Bake at 350°F. for 40 minutes or until hot and bubbly. Top with the tomato and green onion.

KITCHEN tip

*For **2 cups** chopped cooked chicken, in medium saucepan over medium heat, in **4 cups** boiling water, cook **1 pound** skinless, boneless chicken breasts or thighs, cubed, 5 minutes or until chicken is no longer pink. Drain and chop chicken.*

 Family Favorites

Broccoli and Pasta Bianco

MAKES 8 SERVINGS ■ **PREP TIME:** 20 MINUTES ■ **BAKE TIME:** 25 MINUTES

- 6 cups *uncooked* penne pasta
- 4 cups fresh *or* frozen broccoli flowerets
- 1 can (10¾ ounces) Campbell's® Condensed Cream of Mushroom Soup (Regular *or* 98% Fat Free)
- 1½ cups milk
- ½ teaspoon ground black pepper
- 1½ cups shredded mozzarella cheese (about 6 ounces)
- ¼ cup shredded Parmesan cheese

1. Heat the oven to 350°F.

2. Cook the pasta according to the package directions. Add the broccoli for the last 4 minutes of cooking time. Drain the pasta mixture well in a colander.

3. Stir the soup, milk and black pepper in a 2-quart shallow baking dish. Stir in the pasta mixture, ¾ **cup** mozzarella cheese and **2 tablespoons** Parmesan cheese. Top with the remaining mozzarella and Parmesan cheeses.

4. Bake for 25 minutes or until the pasta mixture is hot and bubbling and the cheese is melted.

KITCHEN tip *Creamy white pastas like this one taste great with the tang and heat of crushed red pepper flakes. Serve it on the side.*

Campbell's Family Favorites

Chicken Quesadillas & Fiesta Rice

MAKES 4 SERVINGS ■ **PREP TIME:** 5 MINUTES ■ **COOK TIME:** 15 MINUTES

- 4 skinless, boneless chicken breast halves (about 1 pound), cut into cubes
- 1 can (10¾ ounces) Campbell's® Condensed Cheddar Cheese Soup
- ½ cup Pace® Picante Sauce
- 10 flour tortillas (8-inch), warmed

  Fiesta Rice

1. Heat the oven to 425°F.

2. Cook the chicken in a 10-inch nonstick skillet over medium-high heat until well browned and cooked through, stirring often. Stir in the soup and picante sauce. Cook until the mixture is hot and bubbling.

3. Spread **about ⅓ cup** chicken mixture onto **half** of **each** tortilla to within ½ inch of the edge. Brush the edges of the tortillas with water. Fold the tortillas over the filling and press to seal. Place the filled tortillas onto **2** baking sheets.

4. Bake for 5 minutes or until the quesadillas are hot. Serve with the *Fiesta Rice.*

Fiesta Rice: Heat **1 can** (10 ounces) Campbell's® Condensed Chicken Broth, ½ **cup** water and ½ **cup** Pace® Chunky Salsa in a 1-quart saucepan over medium heat to a boil. Stir in **2 cups uncooked** instant white rice. Cover the saucepan and remove from the heat. Let stand for 5 minutes.

Sliced Steak Pizzaiola

MAKES 6 SERVINGS ▪ **PREP TIME:** 10 MINUTES ▪ **COOK TIME:** 20 MINUTES

- 1 tablespoon vegetable oil
- 1 beef flank steak (about 1½ pounds)
- 2 medium onions, sliced (about 1 cup)
- 2 cloves garlic, minced
- 1 teaspoon Italian seasoning, crushed
- 2 cups Prego® Traditional Italian Sauce *or* Roasted Garlic & Herb Italian Sauce

1. Heat the oil in a 12-inch skillet over medium-high heat. Add the beef and cook for 10 minutes or until it's well browned on both sides. Remove the beef from the skillet. Pour off any fat.

2. Add the onions, garlic and Italian seasoning to the skillet. Cook until the onions are tender. Return the beef to the skillet. Stir in the Italian sauce. Reduce the heat to low. Cook the beef for 3 minutes for medium-rare or to desired doneness.

3. Slice the beef into thin diagonal slices. Serve with the sauce.

French Onion Burgers

MAKES 4 SERVINGS ■ **PREP TIME:** 5 MINUTES ■ **COOK TIME:** 20 MINUTES

- 1 **pound ground beef**
- 1 **can (10½ ounces) Campbell's® Condensed French Onion Soup**
- 4 **slices cheese**
- 4 **Pepperidge Farm® Classic Sandwich Buns with Sesame Seeds, split**

1. Shape the beef into **4** (½-inch-thick) burgers.

2. Heat a 10-inch skillet over medium-high heat. Add the burgers and cook until well browned on both sides. Remove the burgers from the skillet. Pour off any fat.

3. Stir the soup in the skillet and heat to a boil. Return the burgers to the skillet. Reduce the heat to low. Cover and cook for 5 minutes or until desired doneness. Top the burgers with the cheese and cook until the cheese is melted. Serve the burgers on the buns with the soup mixture for dipping.

KITCHEN

You can also serve these burgers in a bowl atop a mound of hot mashed potatoes with some of the soup mixture poured over.

Apple Strudel

MAKES 6 SERVINGS ■ **THAW TIME:** 40 MINUTES ■ **PREP TIME:** 30 MINUTES
BAKE TIME: 35 MINUTES ■ **COOL TIME:** 20 MINUTES

- 1   egg
- 1   tablespoon water
- 2   tablespoons granulated sugar
- 1   tablespoon all-purpose flour
- ¼   teaspoon ground cinnamon
- 2   large Granny Smith apples, peeled, cored and thinly sliced
- 2   tablespoons raisins
- ½   of a 17.3-ounce package Pepperidge Farm® Puff Pastry Sheets (1 sheet), thawed
-     Confectioners' sugar (optional)

1. Heat the oven to 375°F. Beat the egg and water in a small bowl with a fork or whisk. Stir the granulated sugar, flour and cinnamon in a medium bowl. Add the apples and raisins and toss to coat.

2. Unfold the pastry sheet on a lightly floured surface. Roll the pastry sheet into a 16×12-inch rectangle. With the short side facing you, spoon the apple mixture onto the bottom half of the pastry sheet to within 1 inch of the edge. Roll up like a jelly roll. Place seam-side down onto a baking sheet. Tuck the ends under to seal. Brush the pastry with the egg mixture. Cut several slits in the top of the pastry.

3. Bake for 35 minutes or until the strudel is golden brown. Let the strudel cool on the baking sheet on a wire rack for 20 minutes. Sprinkle with the confectioners' sugar, if desired.

KITCHEN

Toss the apples and raisins until they're evenly coated with the flour mixture. The flour helps to thicken the juices released by the apples as they cook.

Family Favorites

Beefy Cornbread Casserole

MAKES 4 SERVINGS ▓ **PREP TIME:** 15 MINUTES ▓ **BAKE TIME:** 25 MINUTES

- 1 **pound ground beef**
- 1 **can (about 15 ounces) red kidney beans, rinsed and drained**
- 1 **can (10¼ ounces) Campbell's® Beef Gravy**
- ½ **cup barbecue sauce**
- 1 **box (about 8 ounces) corn muffin mix**

1. Heat the oven to 375°F. Cook the beef in a 10-inch skillet over medium-high heat until well browned, stirring often to separate the meat. Pour off any fat.

2. Stir the beans, gravy and barbecue sauce in the skillet. Pour the beef mixture into a 2-quart shallow baking dish. Mix the corn muffin mix according to the package directions. Drop the batter by spoonfuls onto the beef mixture.

3. Bake for 25 minutes or until the topping is golden brown.

KITCHEN tip

You can substitute bulk pork sausage for the beef.

Creamy Irish Potato Soup

MAKES 5 SERVINGS ▪ **PREP TIME:** 15 MINUTES ▪ **COOK TIME:** 25 MINUTES

2	tablespoons butter
4	medium green onions, sliced (about ½ cup)
1	stalk celery, sliced (about ½ cup)
1¾	cups Swanson® Chicken Broth (Regular, Natural Goodness® *or* Certified Organic)
⅛	teaspoon ground black pepper
3	medium potatoes, sliced ¼-inch thick (about 3 cups)
1½	cups milk

1. Heat the butter in a 3-quart saucepan over medium heat. Add the onions and celery and cook until they're tender.

2. Stir the broth, black pepper and potatoes in the saucepan and heat to a boil. Reduce the heat to low. Cover and cook for 15 minutes or until the potatoes are tender.

3. Place **half** of the broth mixture and **half** of the milk in a blender or food processor. Cover and blend until smooth. Repeat with the remaining broth mixture and remaining milk. Return to the saucepan and heat through.

Golden Chicken & Autumn Vegetables

MAKES 4 SERVINGS ■ **PREP TIME:** 10 MINUTES ■ **COOK TIME:** 30 MINUTES

1	tablespoon vegetable oil
4	skinless, boneless chicken breast halves (about 1 pound)
1	cup Swanson® Chicken Stock
2	tablespoons minced garlic
½	teaspoon dried rosemary leaves, crushed
½	teaspoon dried thyme leaves, crushed
¼	teaspoon ground black pepper
2	large sweet potatoes, cut into ½-inch pieces
2	cups fresh *or* frozen whole green beans

1. Heat the oil in a 12-inch skillet over medium-high heat. Add the chicken and cook for 10 minutes or until it's well browned on both sides. Remove the chicken from the skillet.

2. Stir the stock, garlic, rosemary, thyme, black pepper, potatoes and green beans in the skillet and heat to a boil. Cook for 5 minutes.

3. Reduce the heat to low. Return the chicken to the skillet. Cover and cook for 10 minutes or until the chicken is cooked through and the potatoes are tender. Season as desired.

Herbed Chicken Dijon with Wine: Add ¼ **cup** white wine, **1 teaspoon** lemon juice and **2 tablespoons** Dijon-style mustard with the stock in step 2. Substitute Yukon Gold potatoes for the sweet potatoes.

KITCHEN tip *You can substitute **4** bone-in chicken breast halves, skin removed (about 2 pounds) for the skinless, boneless chicken. Increase the cooking time to 20 minutes or until the chicken is cooked through.*

 Family Favorites

Seafood Tomato Alfredo

MAKES 4 SERVINGS ▪ **PREP TIME:** 15 MINUTES ▪ **COOK TIME:** 20 MINUTES

- 1 tablespoon butter
- 1 medium onion, chopped (about ½ cup)
- 1 can (10¾ ounces) Campbell's® Condensed Cream of Mushroom with Roasted Garlic Soup
- ½ cup milk
- 1 cup diced canned tomatoes
- 4 fresh fish fillets (flounder, haddock *or* halibut) (about 1 pound), cut into 2-inch pieces
- ½ package (8 ounces) linguine, cooked and drained

1. Heat the butter in a 10-inch skillet over medium heat. Add the onion and cook until tender, stirring occasionally.

2. Stir the soup, milk and tomatoes in the skillet and heat to a boil. Add the fish to the skillet. Reduce the heat to low. Cover and cook for 10 minutes or until the fish flakes easily when tested with a fork. Serve the fish and sauce over the linguine.

Campbell's Family Favorites

Paprika Chicken with Sour Cream Gravy

MAKES 4 SERVINGS ■ **PREP TIME:** 10 MINUTES ■ **COOK TIME:** 20 MINUTES

½   **cup all-purpose flour**

2   **teaspoons paprika**

1   **teaspoon garlic powder**

1   **teaspoon ground black pepper**

1   **teaspoon ground red pepper**

4   **skinless, boneless chicken breast halves (about 1 pound)**

¼   **cup (½ stick) butter**

1   **can (10¾ ounces) Campbell's® Condensed Cream of Chicken Soup (Regular *or* 98% Fat Free)**

2   **green onions, sliced (about ¼ cup)**

1   **container (8 ounces) sour cream**

1. Stir the flour, paprika, garlic powder, black pepper and red pepper on a plate. Coat the chicken with the paprika mixture.

2. Heat the butter in a 10-inch skillet over medium-high heat. Cook the chicken for 10 minutes or until well browned on both sides. Remove the chicken from the skillet.

3. Stir the soup and green onions in the skillet and heat to a boil. Return the chicken to the skillet. Reduce the heat to low. Cover and cook for 5 minutes or until the chicken is cooked through. Stir in the sour cream.

Garlic Mashed Potatoes & Beef Bake

MAKES 4 SERVINGS ▪ **PREP TIME:** 15 MINUTES ▪ **BAKE TIME:** 20 MINUTES

1   **pound ground beef**

1   **can (10¾ ounces) Campbell's® Condensed Cream of Mushroom with Roasted Garlic Soup**

1   **tablespoon Worcestershire sauce**

1   **bag (16 ounces) frozen vegetable combination (broccoli, cauliflower, carrots), thawed**

2   **cups water**

3   **tablespoons butter**

¾   **cup milk**

2   **cups instant mashed potato flakes**

KITCHEN tip

You can use your favorite frozen vegetable combination in this recipe.

1. Heat the oven to 400°F. Cook the beef in a 10-inch skillet over medium-high heat until well browned, stirring often to separate the meat. Pour off any fat.

2. Stir the beef, ½ **can** soup, Worcestershire and vegetables in a 2-quart shallow baking dish.

3. Heat the water, butter and remaining soup in a 3-quart saucepan over medium heat to a boil. Remove the saucepan from the heat. Stir in the milk. Stir in the potatoes. Spoon the potatoes over the beef mixture.

4. Bake for 20 minutes or until the potatoes are lightly browned.

 Family Favorites

Tuscan Sausage and Rigatoni

MAKES 8 SERVINGS ■ **PREP TIME:** 5 MINUTES ■ **COOK TIME:** 20 MINUTES

- 1 pound sweet *or* hot Italian pork sausage, casing removed
- 1 package (8 ounces) sliced mushrooms
- 1 cup frozen peas
- 2⅔ cups Prego® Traditional *or* Marinara Italian Sauce
- 1 package (16 ounces) large tube-shaped pasta (rigatoni) (about 6 cups), cooked and drained
- ⅓ cup grated Parmesan cheese

1. Cook the sausage in a 10-inch skillet over medium-high heat until it's well browned, stirring often to separate the meat. Pour off any fat.

2. Stir the mushrooms and peas in the skillet. Cook for 5 minutes or until the mushrooms are tender, stirring often.

3. Stir the Italian sauce in the skillet. Reduce the heat to medium. Cook until the mixture is hot and bubbling, stirring occasionally.

4. Place the pasta into a large serving bowl. Pour the sausage mixture over the pasta and toss to coat. Top with the cheese.

Creamy Pork Sauté

MAKES 4 SERVINGS ▓ **PREP TIME:** 10 MINUTES ▓ **COOK TIME:** 25 MINUTES

- 2 tablespoons vegetable oil
- 1 boneless pork loin (about 1 pound), cut into thin strips
- 2 stalks celery, sliced (about 1 cup)
- 1 medium onion, chopped (about ½ cup)
- ½ teaspoon dried thyme leaves, crushed
- 1 can (10¾ ounces) Campbell's® Condensed Cream of Celery Soup (Regular *or* 98% Fat Free)
- ¼ cup water

   Hot cooked regular long-grain white rice

1. Heat **1 tablespoon** oil in a 10-inch skillet over medium-high heat. Add the pork and cook until well browned, stirring often. Remove the pork from the skillet.

2. Heat the remaining oil over medium heat. Add the celery, onion and thyme and cook until the vegetables are tender, stirring often.

3. Stir the soup and water in the skillet and heat to a boil. Return the pork to the skillet and cook until the pork is cooked through. Serve the pork mixture over the rice.

Bread and Butter Pudding

MAKES 8 SERVINGS ■ **PREP TIME:** 20 MINUTES ■ **STAND TIME:** 5 MINUTES
BAKE TIME: 40 MINUTES

- ½ cup (1 stick) butter, softened
- 1 loaf (16 ounces) Pepperidge Farm® Toasting White Bread
- 2 teaspoons ground cinnamon
- ¼ cup currants
- 6 eggs
- 2 egg yolks
- ½ cup granulated sugar
- 4 cups heavy cream
- 2 cups milk
- 1 teaspoon vanilla extract
- 2 tablespoons packed brown sugar

1. Heat the oven to 350°F. Grease a 3-quart shallow baking dish with **2 tablespoons** butter.

2. Spread the remaining butter on the bread slices. Cut the bread slices in half diagonally. Arrange **half** the bread slices in the baking dish, overlapping as needed. Sprinkle with **half** the cinnamon and **half** the currants. Repeat with the remaining bread slices, cinnamon and currants.

3. Beat the eggs, egg yolks and granulated sugar in a large bowl with a fork or whisk. Heat the cream and milk in a 2-quart saucepan over low heat until the mixture is warm. Stir in the vanilla extract. Stir some of the cream mixture into the egg mixture. Stir the egg mixture in the saucepan.

4. Pour the egg mixture over the bread. Let stand for 5 minutes. Sprinkle with the brown sugar.

5. Bake for 40 minutes or until set.

Make Ahead: Prepare the recipe as directed above but do not bake. Cover and refrigerate overnight. Bake at 350°F. for 40 minutes or until set.

Breakfast Pizza

MAKES 6 SERVINGS ■ **PREP TIME:** 20 MINUTES ■ **COOK TIME:** 10 MINUTES
BAKE TIME: 5 MINUTES

- 1 tablespoon butter
- ¼ cup chopped onion
- ¼ cup chopped green pepper
- ¼ cup chopped Canadian bacon
- 1 (12-inch) prepared pizza crust
- 8 eggs, beaten
- ¼ teaspoon ground black pepper
- ¾ cup Pace® Picante Sauce
- 2 ounces shredded Cheddar cheese (about ½ cup)
- 2 tablespoons chopped fresh cilantro leaves

1. Heat the oven to 400°F.

2. Heat the butter in a 10-inch skillet over medium heat. Add the onion, green pepper and bacon and cook until the vegetables are tender.

3. Place the pizza crust onto a pizza pan or baking sheet. Place in the oven to warm.

4. Stir the eggs and black pepper in the skillet. Cook and stir until the eggs are set. Spoon the egg mixture onto the pizza crust. Top with the picante sauce. Sprinkle with the cheese.

5. Bake for 5 minutes or until the cheese is melted. Sprinkle with the cilantro. Cut the pizza into **6** slices.

Cincinnati Chili

MAKES 8 SERVINGS ■ **PREP TIME:** 10 MINUTES ■ **COOK TIME:** 1 HOUR

1½   pounds ground beef

  2   large onions, chopped (about 2 cups)

  ¼   teaspoon garlic powder *or* 2 cloves garlic, minced

  2   teaspoons chili powder

  ¼   teaspoon ground cinnamon

       Dash ground cloves

  4   cups Campbell's® Tomato Juice

  2   cans (about 15 ounces *each*) kidney beans, drained

       Hot cooked spaghetti

1. Cook beef, onions and garlic powder in saucepot over medium-high heat in 2 batches until beef is browned and onion is tender, stirring to separate the meat. Remove beef and onion. Pour off any fat. Return beef and onion to saucepot.

2. Stir in chili powder, cinnamon and cloves and cook 2 minutes. Stir in tomato juice. Heat to a boil. Cover and cook over low heat 30 minutes.

3. Add beans. Cover and cook 15 minutes, stirring occasionally. Serve over spaghetti.

Chicken & Broccoli Alfredo

MAKES 4 SERVINGS ▪ **PREP TIME:** 10 MINUTES ▪ **COOK TIME:** 20 MINUTES

½ of a 16-ounce package linguine

1 cup fresh *or* frozen broccoli flowerets

2 tablespoons butter

4 skinless, boneless chicken breast halves (about 1 pound), cut into 1½-inch pieces

1 can (10¾ ounces) Campbell's® Condensed Cream of Mushroom Soup (Regular, 98% Fat Free *or* Healthy Request®)

½ cup milk

½ cup grated Parmesan cheese

¼ teaspoon ground black pepper

1. Prepare the linguine according to the package directions in a 3-quart saucepan. Add the broccoli during the last 4 minutes of the cooking time. Drain the linguine mixture well in a colander.

2. Heat the butter in a 10-inch skillet over medium-high heat. Add the chicken and cook until it's well browned, stirring often.

3. Stir the soup, milk, cheese, black pepper and linguine mixture in the skillet and cook until the chicken is cooked through, stirring occasionally. Serve with additional Parmesan cheese.

KITCHEN tip

You can substitute spaghetti or fettuccine for the linguine in this recipe.

Grilled Chicken & Broccoli Alfredo: Substitute grilled chicken breasts for the skinless, boneless chicken.

Shrimp & Broccoli Alfredo: Substitute **1 pound** fresh extra large shrimp, shelled and deveined, for the chicken. Cook as directed for the chicken above, until the shrimp are cooked through.

 Family Favorites

Cheesy Enchilada Stack

MAKES 8 SERVINGS ■ **PREP TIME:** 20 MINUTES ■ **BAKE TIME:** 45 MINUTES

- 1 **pound ground beef**
- 2 **cups prepared enchilada sauce**
  Vegetable cooking spray
- 6 **flour tortillas (10-inch)**
- 8 **ounces shredded Cheddar cheese (about 2 cups)**
- 1 **can (about 16 ounces) refried beans**
- 2 **cans (4 ounces *each*) chopped green chiles, drained**
  Chopped green onions

1. Cook the beef in a 10-inch skillet over medium-high heat until it's well browned, stirring often to separate the meat. Pour off any fat. Stir ½ **cup** of the enchilada sauce in the skillet. Spray a baking sheet with the cooking spray.

2. Place **1** tortilla onto the baking sheet. Top with ⅓ of the beef mixture and ¼ **cup** cheese. Top with **1** tortilla, ½ of the refried beans, ½ **cup** enchilada sauce, **1 can** chiles and ¼ **cup** cheese. Repeat the layers. Top with **1** tortilla, remaining beef mixture and ¼ **cup** cheese. Top with the remaining tortilla. Cover the stack with aluminum foil.

3. Bake at 400°F. for 40 minutes or until the filling is hot. Uncover the stack. Top with the remaining enchilada sauce, cheese and onions. Bake for 5 minutes or until the cheese is melted. Cut the stack into **8** wedges.

 Family Favorites

Now & Later Baked Ziti

2	pounds ground beef
1	large onion, chopped (about 1 cup)
7½	cups Prego® Fresh Mushroom Italian Sauce
9	cups tube-shaped pasta (ziti), cooked and drained
12	ounces shredded mozzarella cheese (about 3 cups)
½	cup grated Parmesan cheese

1. Cook the beef and onion in an 8-quart saucepot over medium-high heat until the beef is well browned, stirring often to separate the meat. Pour off any fat.

2. Stir the Italian sauce, ziti and **2 cups** mozzarella cheese in the saucepot. Spoon the beef mixture into **2** (12½×8½×2-inch) disposable foil pans. Top with the remaining mozzarella and Parmesan cheeses.

3. Bake at 350°F. for 30 minutes or until the beef mixture is hot and the cheese is melted.

KITCHEN tip

To make ahead and freeze, prepare the ziti as directed above but do not bake. Cover the pans with foil and freeze. Bake the frozen ziti, uncovered, at 350°F. for 1 hour or until it's hot. Or, thaw the ziti in the refrigerator for 24 hours, then bake, uncovered, at 350°F. for 45 minutes or until it's hot.

Sensational Chicken Noodle Soup

MAKES 4 SERVINGS ■ **PREP TIME:** 5 MINUTES ■ **COOK TIME:** 25 MINUTES

4 cups Swanson® Chicken Broth (Regular, Natural Goodness® *or* Certified Organic)

Generous dash ground black pepper

1 medium carrot, sliced (about ½ cup)

1 stalk celery, sliced (about ½ cup)

½ cup *uncooked* extra-wide egg noodles

1 cup shredded cooked chicken *or* turkey

1. Heat the broth, black pepper, carrot and celery in a 2-quart saucepan over medium-high heat to a boil.

2. Stir the noodles and chicken into the saucepan. Reduce the heat to medium. Cook for 10 minutes or until the noodles are tender.

Asian Soup: Add **2** green onions cut into ½-inch pieces, **1 clove** garlic, minced, **1 teaspoon** ground ginger and **2 teaspoons** soy sauce. Substitute **uncooked** curly Asian noodles for egg noodles.

Mexican Soup: Add ½ **cup** Pace® Chunky Salsa, **1 clove** garlic, minced, **1 cup** rinsed and drained black beans and ½ **teaspoon** chili powder. Substitute **2** corn tortillas (4 or 6-inch) cut into thin strips for the noodles, adding them just before serving.

Italian Tortellini Soup: Add **1 can** (about 14.5 ounces) diced tomatoes, drained, **1 clove** garlic, minced, **1 teaspoon** dried Italian seasoning, crushed, and **1 cup** spinach leaves. Substitute ½ **cup** frozen cheese tortellini for egg noodles. Serve with grated Parmesan cheese.

Chicken & Stir-Fry Vegetable Pizza

MAKES 4 SERVINGS ▪ **PREP TIME:** 5 MINUTES ▪ **COOK TIME:** 5 MINUTES
BAKE TIME: 10 MINUTES

1	can (10¾ ounces) Campbell's® Condensed Cream of Mushroom Soup (Regular *or* 98% Fat Free)
1	prepared pizza crust (12-inch)
1	tablespoon vegetable oil
3	cups frozen vegetables
⅛	teaspoon garlic powder
1	package (about 10 ounces) refrigerated cooked chicken strips
1	cup shredded Cheddar cheese (about 4 ounces)
	Dried oregano leaves

1. Spread the soup on the crust to within ¼ inch of the edge. Bake at 450°F. for 5 minutes.

2. Heat the oil in a 10-inch skillet over medium heat. Add the vegetables and garlic and cook until the vegetables are tender-crisp, stirring occasionally.

3. Spoon the vegetables on the pizza. Top with the chicken and cheese. Sprinkle with the oregano, if desired.

4. Bake for 5 minutes or until the cheese is melted.

Campbell's Family Favorites

Shortcut Ravioli Lasagna

MAKES 6 SERVINGS ▓ **PREP TIME:** 10 MINUTES ▓ **BAKE TIME:** 45 MINUTES
STAND TIME: 10 MINUTES

Vegetable cooking spray

3   cups Prego® Italian Sausage & Garlic Italian Sauce

½   cup water

1   package (30 ounces) frozen regular-size cheese-filled ravioli
(about 30 to 34)

1½   cups shredded mozzarella cheese (about 6 ounces)

Grated Parmesan cheese *and* chopped fresh parsley

1. Heat the oven to 375°F. Spray a 13×9×2-inch baking dish with the cooking spray.

2. Stir the Italian sauce and water in a medium bowl. Spread **1 cup** sauce mixture in the baking dish. Top with ½ of the ravioli, **¾ cup** mozzarella cheese and **1 cup** sauce mixture. Top with the remaining ravioli and sauce mixture. Cover the baking dish.

3. Bake for 35 minutes or until the mixture is hot and bubbling. Uncover the baking dish. Sprinkle with the remaining mozzarella cheese.

4. Bake for 10 minutes or until the cheese is melted. Let stand for 10 minutes. Garnish with the Parmesan cheese and parsley.

Amazing Red Devil's Food Cake

MAKES 12 SERVINGS ▪ **PREP TIME:** 15 MINUTES ▪ **BAKE TIME:** 35 MINUTES
COOL TIME: 40 MINUTES

- 2½ cups all-purpose flour
- ½ cup unsweetened cocoa powder
- 1½ teaspoons baking soda
- ¼ teaspoon salt
- ½ cup (1 stick) butter, softened
- 1¾ cups sugar
- 2 eggs
- 1 teaspoon vanilla extract
- 1½ cups Campbell's® Tomato Juice
- *Creamy Butter Frosting*

1. Heat the oven to 350°F. Grease and flour **2** (8-inch) round cake pans.

2. Stir the flour, cocoa, baking soda and salt in a medium bowl.

3. Beat the butter and sugar in a large bowl with an electric mixer on medium speed until the mixture is light and fluffy. Beat in the eggs, one at a time, beating well after each addition. Beat in the vanilla extract.

4. Reduce the speed to low. Add the flour mixture alternately with the tomato juice, beating well after each addition. Pour the batter into the cake pans.

5. Bake for 35 minutes or until a toothpick inserted in the center comes out clean. Cool the cakes in the pans on wire racks for 10 minutes. Remove the cakes from the pans and cool completely on the wire racks. Frost and fill with the *Creamy Butter Frosting*. Refrigerate until ready to serve.

 Family Favorites

Creamy Butter Frosting: Place ¾ **cup** (1½ sticks) butter, softened, **1 package** (16 ounces) confectioners' sugar, ¼ **cup** milk, ½ **teaspoon** vanilla extract and ¼ **teaspoon** salt in a medium bowl. Beat with an electric mixer on low speed until the mixture is smooth. Increase the speed to medium, adding more milk, if needed, until desired consistency. Makes 2½ cups.

Classic Tuna Noodle Casserole

MAKES 4 SERVINGS ■ **PREP TIME:** 10 MINUTES ■ **BAKE TIME:** 25 MINUTES

1 can (10¾ ounces) Campbell's® Condensed Cream of Celery Soup (Regular *or* 98% Fat Free)

½ cup milk

1 cup cooked peas

2 tablespoons chopped pimientos

2 cans (about 6 ounces *each*) tuna, drained and flaked

2 cups hot cooked medium egg noodles

2 tablespoons dry bread crumbs

1 tablespoon butter, melted

1. Heat the oven to 400°F. Stir the soup, milk, peas, pimientos, tuna and noodles in a 1½-quart baking dish. Stir the bread crumbs and butter in a small bowl.

2. Bake for 20 minutes or until the tuna mixture is hot and bubbling. Stir the tuna mixture. Sprinkle with the bread crumb mixture.

3. Bake for 5 minutes or until the bread crumbs are golden brown.

KITCHEN tip

Substitute Campbell's® Condensed Cream of Mushroom Soup for the Cream of Celery.

To melt the butter, remove the wrapper and place the butter into a microwavable cup. Cover and microwave on HIGH for 30 seconds.

Campbell's Family Favorites

Chicken Crunch

MAKES 4 SERVINGS ■ **PREP TIME:** 10 MINUTES ■ **BAKE TIME:** 20 MINUTES
COOK TIME: 5 MINUTES

1	can (10¾ ounces) Campbell's® Condensed Cream of Chicken Soup (Regular *or* 98% Fat Free)
½	cup milk
4	skinless, boneless chicken breast halves (about 1 pound)
2	tablespoons all-purpose flour
1½	cups Pepperidge Farm® Herb Seasoned Stuffing, finely crushed
2	tablespoons butter, melted

1. Heat the oven to 400°F. Stir ⅓ **cup** soup and ¼ **cup** milk in a shallow dish. Coat the chicken with the flour. Dip the chicken in the soup mixture. Coat the chicken with the stuffing. Place the chicken onto a baking sheet. Drizzle with the butter.

2. Bake for 20 minutes or until the chicken is cooked through.

3. Heat the remaining soup and milk in a 1-quart saucepan over medium-high heat until the mixture is hot and bubbling. Serve the sauce with the chicken.

Mexican Pizza

MAKES 4 SERVINGS ▓ **THAW TIME:** 40 MINUTES ▓ **PREP TIME:** 20 MINUTES
BAKE TIME: 15 MINUTES

- ½ of a 17.3-ounce package Pepperidge Farm® Puff Pastry Sheets (1 sheet), thawed
- ¾ cup Prego® Traditional Italian Sauce
- ¼ cup Pace® Picante Sauce
- ¾ cup shredded mozzarella cheese
- ¾ cup shredded Cheddar cheese
- ¼ cup sliced pitted ripe olives

1. Heat the oven to 400°F.

2. Unfold the pastry sheet on a lightly floured surface. Roll the pastry sheet into a 15×10-inch rectangle. Place the pastry onto a baking sheet. Prick the pastry thoroughly with a fork. Bake for 10 minutes or until the pastry is golden brown.

3. Stir the Italian sauce and picante sauce in a small bowl. Spread the sauce mixture on the pastry to within ½ inch of the edge. Top with the cheeses and sprinkle with the olives. Bake for 5 minutes or until the cheese is melted.

Slow Cooker Hearty Beef Stew

MAKES 6 SERVINGS ■ **PREP TIME:** 20 MINUTES
COOK TIME: 10 HOURS 15 MINUTES

1½	pounds beef for stew, cut into 1-inch pieces
	Ground black pepper
¼	cup all-purpose flour
1	tablespoon vegetable oil
1	pound medium potatoes, cut into cubes (about 3 cups)
4	medium carrots, sliced (about 2 cups)
2	medium onions, cut into wedges
4	cloves garlic, minced
3¼	cups Swanson® Beef Stock
1	tablespoon Worcestershire sauce
1	teaspoon dried thyme leaves, crushed
1	bay leaf
1	cup thawed frozen peas

1. Season the beef with black pepper. Coat the beef with **2 tablespoons** of the flour. Heat the oil in a 10-inch skillet over medium-high heat. Add the beef in 2 batches and cook until it's well browned, stirring often.

2. Place the potatoes, carrots, onions and garlic into a 5-quart slow cooker. Top with the beef. Add **3 cups** of the stock, Worcestershire, thyme and bay leaf.

3. Cover and cook on LOW for 10 to 11 hours* or until the beef is fork-tender. Remove and discard the bay leaf.

 Family Favorites

4. Stir the remaining flour and stock in a small bowl until the mixture is smooth. Stir the flour mixture and peas in the cooker. Increase the heat to HIGH. Cover and cook for 15 minutes or until the mixture boils and thickens.

Or on HIGH for 5 to 6 hours.

Southwest Skillet

MAKES 4 SERVINGS ▪ **PREP TIME:** 5 MINUTES ▪ **COOK TIME:** 20 MINUTES
STAND TIME: 5 MINUTES

- ¾ **pound ground beef**
- 1 **tablespoon chili powder**
- 1 **can (10¾ ounces) Campbell's® Condensed Beefy Mushroom Soup**
- ¼ **cup water**
- 1 **can (14.5 ounces) whole peeled tomatoes, cut up**
- 1 **can (about 15 ounces) kidney beans, rinsed and drained**
- ¾ **cup *uncooked* instant rice**
- ½ **cup shredded Cheddar cheese (2 ounces)**
   Tortilla chips

1. Cook the beef with chili powder in a 10-inch skillet over medium-high heat until the beef is well browned, stirring frequently to separate the meat. Pour off any fat.

2. Stir the soup, water, tomatoes and beans into the skillet. Heat to a boil. Reduce the heat to low. Cover and cook for 10 minutes.

3. Stir the rice into the skillet. Cover the skillet and remove from the heat. Let stand for 5 minutes. Top with the cheese. Serve with the chips.

Campbell's Family Favorites

Creamy Chicken Tortilla Soup

MAKES 6 SERVINGS ▪ **PREP TIME:** 15 MINUTES

COOK TIME: 4 HOURS 15 MINUTES

- 1 cup Pace® Picante Sauce
- 2 cans (10¾ ounces *each*) Campbell's® Condensed Cream of Chicken Soup
- 1 pound skinless, boneless chicken breasts, cut into ½-inch pieces
- 2 cups frozen whole kernel corn
- 1 can (about 15 ounces) black beans, rinsed and drained
- 1 soup can water
- 1 teaspoon ground cumin
- 4 corn tortillas (6-inch), cut into strips
- 1 cup shredded Cheddar cheese (about 4 ounces)
- ⅓ cup chopped fresh cilantro leaves

1. Stir the picante sauce, soup, chicken, corn, beans, water and cumin in a 4-quart slow cooker.

2. Cover and cook on LOW for 4 to 5 hours* or until the chicken is cooked through.

3. Stir the tortillas, cheese and cilantro into the cooker. Cover and cook for 15 minutes. Serve with additional cheese, if desired.

Or on HIGH for 2 to 2½ hours.

Weekday Pot Roast & Vegetables

MAKES 8 SERVINGS ▪ **PREP TIME:** 15 MINUTES ▪ **COOK TIME:** 10 HOURS

- 1 boneless beef bottom round roast *or* chuck pot roast (2 to 2½ pounds)
- 1 teaspoon garlic powder
- 1 tablespoon vegetable oil
- 1 pound potatoes, cut into wedges
- 3 cups fresh *or* frozen whole baby carrots
- 1 medium onion, thickly sliced (about ¾ cup)
- 2 teaspoons dried basil leaves, crushed
- 2 cans (10¼ ounces *each*) Campbell's® Beef Gravy

1. Season the beef with the garlic powder. Heat the oil in a 10-inch skillet over medium-high heat. Add the beef and cook until well browned on all sides.

2. Place the potatoes, carrots and onion into a 3½-quart slow cooker. Sprinkle with the basil. Add the beef to the cooker. Pour the gravy over the beef and vegetables.

3. Cover and cook on LOW for 10 to 11 hours* or until the beef is fork-tender.

Or on HIGH for 5 to 6 hours.

 Family Favorites

Oven-Fried Chicken Chimichangas

MAKES 6 SERVINGS ▪ **PREP TIME:** 20 MINUTES ▪ **BAKE TIME:** 25 MINUTES

- ⅔ cup Pace® Picante Sauce
- 1 teaspoon ground cumin
- ½ teaspoon dried oregano leaves, crushed
- 1½ cups chopped cooked chicken
- 4 ounces shredded Cheddar cheese (about 1 cup)
- 2 green onions, chopped (about ¼ cup)
- 6 flour tortillas (8-inch)
- 2 tablespoons butter, melted
  Fresh cilantro leaves

1. Stir the picante sauce, cumin, oregano, chicken, cheese and onions in a medium bowl.

2. Place **about ½ cup** of the chicken mixture in the center of **each** tortilla. Fold the opposite sides over the filling. Roll up from the bottom and place seam-side down on a baking sheet. Brush with butter.

3. Bake at 400°F. for 25 minutes or until they're golden brown. Serve with additional picante sauce. Garnish with cilantro.

KITCHEN tip

*For **1½ cups** chopped chicken, in a 2-quart saucepan over medium heat, in **4 cups** boiling water, cook ¾ **pound** boneless chicken breasts **or** thighs, cubed, for 5 minutes or until the chicken is cooked through. Drain and chop the chicken.*

Creamy Chicken Florentine

MAKES 4 SERVINGS ▪ **PREP TIME:** 15 MINUTES ▪ **BAKE TIME:** 40 MINUTES
STAND TIME: 5 MINUTES

1	can (10¾ ounces) Campbell's® Condensed Cream of Chicken Soup (Regular *or* 98% Fat Free)
1½	cups water
½	of a 20-ounce bag frozen cut leaf spinach, thawed and well drained (about 3½ cups)
1	can (about 14.5 ounces) Italian-style diced tomatoes
4	skinless, boneless chicken breast halves (about 1 pound), cut into 1-inch cubes
2½	cups *uncooked* penne pasta
½	cup shredded mozzarella cheese

1. Heat the oven to 375°F. Stir the soup, water, spinach, tomatoes and chicken in a 3-quart shallow baking dish. Cover the baking dish.

2. Bake for 20 minutes. Cook the pasta according to the package directions and drain well in a colander. Uncover the baking dish and stir in the pasta.

3. Bake for 20 minutes or until the pasta mixture is hot and bubbling. Sprinkle with the cheese. Let stand for 5 minutes or until the cheese is melted.

Chicken Pasta Alfredo

MAKES 4 SERVINGS ▧ **PREP TIME:** 15 MINUTES ▧ **COOK TIME:** 10 MINUTES

4	ounces cream cheese, cut into cubes
1½	cups milk
¾	cup grated Parmesan cheese
1	can (12.5 ounces)* Swanson® Premium White Chunk Chicken Breast in Water, drained
1	cup frozen peas, thawed
½	of a 1-pound package fettuccine, cooked and drained (about 4½ cups)

Or 3 cans (4.5 ounces each).

1. Heat the cream cheese and milk in a 10-inch skillet over medium heat to a boil, stirring constantly. Stir in ½ **cup** Parmesan cheese. Reduce the heat to low. Cook for 5 minutes.

2. Add the chicken, peas and fettuccine to the skillet and toss to coat. Heat through. Sprinkle with the remaining cheese and serve immediately.

KITCHEN tip *For a more traditional Alfredo sauce, substitute **2 tablespoons** butter and **1½ cups** heavy cream for the cream cheese and milk. Proceed with the recipe as directed above.*

Easiest Prep Dishes

*Easy Chicken Paprikash
(recipe page 56)*

Easy Chicken Paprikash

MAKES 4 SERVINGS ■ **PREP TIME:** 10 MINUTES ■ **COOK TIME:** 20 MINUTES

1¾ cups Swanson® Chicken Stock

¼ cup all-purpose flour

2 teaspoons paprika

⅛ teaspoon ground red pepper

4 skinless, boneless chicken breast halves (about 1 pound)

1 medium onion, sliced (about ½ cup)

⅓ cup plain yogurt

4 cups hot cooked egg noodles

1. Stir the stock, flour, paprika and red pepper in a small bowl until the mixture is smooth.

2. Cook the chicken in a 10-inch nonstick skillet over medium-high heat for 10 minutes or until it's well browned on both sides.

3. Add the onion to the skillet. Reduce the heat to medium. Cover and cook until the onion is tender-crisp. Stir in the stock mixture. Cook and stir until the mixture boils and thickens and the chicken is cooked through. Remove the skillet from the heat.

4. Stir in the yogurt. Serve the chicken mixture with the noodles.

Creamy Chicken and Vegetables

MAKES 4 SERVINGS ▪ **PREP TIME:** 5 MINUTES ▪ **COOK TIME:** 20 MINUTES

Vegetable cooking spray

4 skinless, boneless chicken breast halves (about 1 pound)

1 can (10¾ ounces) Campbell's® Healthy Request® Condensed Cream of Mushroom Soup

½ cup milk

1 tablespoon lemon juice

¼ teaspoon dried basil leaves, crushed

⅛ teaspoon garlic powder

1 bag (16 ounces) frozen vegetable combination (broccoli, cauliflower, carrots)

1. Spray a 12-inch skillet with the cooking spray and heat over medium-high heat for 1 minute. Add the chicken and cook until well browned on both sides. Remove the chicken from the skillet.

2. Heat the soup, milk, lemon juice, basil, garlic powder and vegetables in the skillet to a boil. Return the chicken to the skillet. Reduce the heat to low. Cover and cook for 5 minutes or until the chicken is cooked through.

Beef & Mushroom Dijon

MAKES 4 SERVINGS ■ **PREP TIME:** 10 MINUTES ■ **COOK TIME:** 25 MINUTES

Vegetable cooking spray

2 cups sliced mushrooms (about 6 ounces)

1 medium onion, chopped (about ½ cup)

1 boneless beef sirloin steak, ¾-inch thick (about ¾ pound), cut into strips

1 can (10¾ ounces) Campbell's® Condensed Cream of Mushroom Soup (Regular, 98% Fat Free *or* Healthy Request®)

½ cup water

2 tablespoons Dijon-style mustard

4 cups hot cooked rice, cooked without salt

Chopped fresh parsley (optional)

1. Spray a 10-inch skillet with the cooking spray and heat over medium heat for 1 minute. Add the mushrooms and onion and cook until they're tender. Remove the vegetables from the skillet. Remove the skillet from the heat.

2. Spray the skillet with the cooking spray and heat over medium-high heat for 1 minute. Add the beef and cook until it's well browned, stirring often. Pour off any fat.

3. Stir the soup, water, mustard and vegetables in the skillet and cook until the mixture is hot and bubbling. Toss the rice with the parsley, if desired. Serve the beef mixture with the rice.

KITCHEN tip

To make slicing easier, freeze the beef for 1 hour.

Campbell's   Easiest Prep Dishes

Dripping Roast Beef Sandwiches with Melted Provolone

MAKES 4 SERVINGS ▪ **PREP TIME:** 5 MINUTES
COOK TIME: 5 MINUTES ▪ **BAKE TIME:** 3 MINUTES

1	can (10½ ounces) Campbell's® Condensed French Onion Soup
1	tablespoon reduced-sodium Worcestershire sauce
¾	pound thinly sliced deli roast beef
4	Pepperidge Farm® Classic Soft Hoagie Rolls with Sesame Seeds
4	slices deli provolone cheese, cut in half
¼	cup drained hot or mild pickled banana pepper rings

1. Heat the oven to 400°F.

2. Heat the soup and Worcestershire in a 2-quart saucepan over medium-high heat to a boil. Add the beef and heat through, stirring occasionally.

3. Divide the beef evenly among the rolls. Top the beef with the cheese slices and place the sandwiches onto a baking sheet.

4. Bake for 3 minutes or until the sandwiches are toasted and the cheese is melted. Spoon the soup mixture onto the sandwiches. Top **each** sandwich with **1 tablespoon** pepper rings.

KITCHEN

*You may substitute ½ of a **11.25-ounce package** Pepperidge Farm®* *Texas Toast (4 slices), prepared according to package directions, for the rolls in this recipe. Serve the sandwiches open-faced.*

3-Cheese Pasta Bake

MAKES 4 SERVINGS ▪ **PREP TIME:** 20 MINUTES ▪ **BAKE TIME:** 20 MINUTES

1   can (10¾ ounces) Campbell's® Condensed Cream of Mushroom Soup (Regular *or* 98% Fat Free)

1   package (8 ounces) shredded two-cheese blend (about 2 cups)

⅓   cup grated Parmesan cheese

1   cup milk

¼   teaspoon ground black pepper

3   cups corkscrew-shaped pasta (rotini), cooked and drained

1. Stir the soup, cheeses, milk and black pepper in a 1½-quart casserole. Stir in the pasta.

2. Bake at 400°F. for 20 minutes or until the mixture is hot and bubbling.

KITCHEN
tip

*Substitute **2 cups** of your favorite shredded cheese for the two-cheese blend.*

Lemony Olive Chicken

MAKES 4 SERVINGS ▪ **PREP TIME:** 10 MINUTES ▪ **COOK TIME:** 20 MINUTES

- 1 tablespoon vegetable oil
- 4 skinless, boneless chicken breast halves (about 1 pound)
- 1 can (10¾ ounces) Campbell's® Condensed Cream of Chicken Soup (Regular *or* 98% Fat Free)
- ¼ cup milk
- ½ teaspoon lemon juice
- ⅛ teaspoon ground black pepper
- ½ cup sliced pitted ripe olives
- 4 lemon slices
- 4 cups hot cooked rice

1. Heat the oil in a 10-inch skillet over medium-high heat. Add the chicken and cook until well browned on both sides.

2. Stir the soup, milk, lemon juice, black pepper and olives in the skillet and heat to a boil. Top the chicken with the lemon slices. Reduce the heat to low. Cover and cook for 5 minutes or until the chicken is cooked through. Serve the chicken and sauce with the rice.

Sausage and Bean Ragoût

MAKES 6 SERVINGS ▪ **PREP TIME:** 15 MINUTES ▪ **COOK TIME:** 40 MINUTES

- 2 tablespoons olive oil
- 1 pound ground beef
- 1 pound hot Italian pork sausage, casing removed
- 1 large onion, chopped (about 1 cup)
- 4 cloves garlic, minced
- 3½ cups Swanson® Chicken Stock
- ¼ cup chopped fresh basil leaves
- 2 cans (14.5 ounces *each*) Italian-style diced tomatoes
- 1 can (about 15 ounces) white kidney beans (cannellini), rinsed and drained
- ½ cup *uncooked* elbow pasta
- 1 bag (6 ounces) fresh baby spinach leaves
- ⅓ cup grated Romano cheese

1. Heat the oil in a 6-quart saucepot over medium-high heat. Add the beef, sausage and onion and cook until the beef and sausage are well browned, stirring often to separate the meat. Pour off any fat. Add the garlic and cook and stir for 30 seconds.

2. Stir the stock, basil, tomatoes and beans in the saucepot and heat to a boil. Reduce the heat to low. Cover and cook for 10 minutes, stirring occasionally. Add the pasta and cook until it's tender.

KITCHEN tip

This recipe calls for cooking the pasta until it's tender. However, if you like your pasta a little al dente, that will work as well.

3. Stir in the spinach and cook until the spinach is wilted. Remove the saucepot from the heat and stir in the cheese. Serve with additional cheese, if desired.

Campbell's Easiest Prep Dishes

Beef Taco Bake

MAKES 4 SERVINGS ▪ **PREP TIME:** 10 MINUTES ▪ **BAKE TIME:** 30 MINUTES

- 1 **pound ground beef**
- 1 **can (10¾ ounces) Campbell's® Condensed Tomato Soup**
- 1 **cup Pace® Picante Sauce**
- ½ **cup milk**
- 6 **flour tortillas (8-inch) *or* corn tortillas (6-inch), cut into 1-inch pieces**
- 1 **cup shredded Cheddar cheese (about 4 ounces)**

1. Cook the beef in a 10-inch skillet over medium-high heat until well browned, stirring often. Pour off any fat.

2. Stir the soup, picante sauce, milk, tortillas and **half** the cheese in the skillet. Spoon the beef mixture into a 2-quart shallow baking dish. Cover the baking dish.

3. Bake at 400°F. for 30 minutes or until the beef mixture is hot and bubbling. Sprinkle with the remaining cheese.

Garlic Pork Chops

MAKES 4 SERVINGS ▪ **PREP TIME:** 5 MINUTES ▪ **COOK TIME:** 20 MINUTES

- 1   **tablespoon vegetable oil**
- 4   **boneless pork chops, ¾-inch thick (about 1 pound)**
- 1   **clove garlic, minced**
- 1   **can (10¾ ounces) Campbell's® Condensed Cream of Mushroom Soup (Regular *or* 98% Fat Free)**
- ½   **cup milk**
- 4   **cups hot cooked couscous *or* rice**

1. Heat the oil in a 10-inch skillet over medium-high heat. Add the pork chops and garlic and cook for 10 minutes or until the chops are well browned on both sides. Remove the pork chops and set aside.

2. Stir the soup and milk into the skillet. Heat to a boil. Return the pork chops to the skillet and reduce the heat to low. Cover and cook for 5 minutes or until the chops are cooked through. Serve with the couscous or rice.

Quick Skillet Chicken & Macaroni Parmesan

MAKES 6 SERVINGS ■ **PREP TIME:** 15 MINUTES ■ **COOK TIME:** 15 MINUTES
STAND TIME: 5 MINUTES

1	jar (1 pound 10 ounces) Prego® Traditional Italian Sauce
¼	cup grated Parmesan cheese
3	cups cubed cooked chicken
1½	cups elbow macaroni, cooked and drained
1½	cups shredded part-skim mozzarella cheese (6 ounces)

1. Heat the Italian sauce, **3 tablespoons** of the Parmesan cheese, chicken and macaroni in a 10-inch skillet over medium-high heat to a boil. Reduce the heat to medium. Cover and cook for 10 minutes or until the mixture is hot and bubbling, stirring occasionally.

2. Sprinkle with the mozzarella cheese and remaining Parmesan cheese. Let stand for 5 minutes or until the cheese melts.

KITCHEN

Use 1½ pounds skinless, boneless chicken breasts, cut into cubes, for the cooked chicken. Heat 1 tablespoon olive oil in a 12-inch skillet over medium-high heat. Add the chicken in 2 batches and cook until it's well browned, stirring often. Continue to cook, proceeding as directed in step 1 above.

Campbell's Easiest Prep Dishes

Creamy Ranch Pork Chops & Rice

MAKES 4 SERVINGS ■ **PREP TIME:** 5 MINUTES ■ **COOK TIME:** 25 MINUTES

- 1 tablespoon vegetable oil
- 4 boneless pork chops, ¾-inch thick (about 1 pound)
- 1 can (10¾ ounces) Campbell's® Condensed Cream of Mushroom Soup (Regular *or* 98% Fat Free)
- ¾ cup milk
- 1 package (1 ounce) ranch salad dressing mix
- Paprika
- *Ranch-Style Rice*

1. Heat the oil in a 10-inch skillet over medium-high heat. Add the pork and cook until well browned on both sides.

2. Stir the soup, milk and ½ **package** salad dressing mix in the skillet and heat to a boil. Reduce the heat to low. Cover and cook for 10 minutes or until the pork is cooked through. Sprinkle with the paprika.

3. Serve with the *Ranch-Style Rice*.

Ranch-Style Rice: Heat **2¼ cups** water and the remaining salad dressing mix in a 3-quart saucepan over medium-high heat to a boil. Stir in **1 cup uncooked** regular long-grain white rice and cook according to the package directions.

Skillet Herb Roasted Chicken

MAKES 4 SERVINGS ■ **PREP TIME:** 10 MINUTES ■ **COOK TIME:** 20 MINUTES

- 2 tablespoons all-purpose flour
- ¼ teaspoon ground sage
- ¼ teaspoon dried thyme leaves, crushed
- 4 skinless, boneless chicken breast halves (about 1 pound)
- 2 tablespoons butter
- 1 can (10¾ ounces) Campbell's® Condensed Cream of Chicken Soup (Regular *or* 98% Fat Free)
- ½ cup water
- 4 cups hot cooked rice

1. Stir the flour, sage and thyme on a plate. Coat the chicken with the flour mixture.

2. Heat the butter in a 10-inch skillet over medium-high heat. Add the chicken and cook for 15 minutes or until well browned on both sides and cooked through. Remove the chicken from the skillet and keep warm.

3. Stir the soup and water in the skillet and cook until the mixture is hot and bubbling. Serve the sauce with the chicken and rice.

Broth Simmered Rice

MAKES 4 SERVINGS ▪ **PREP TIME:** 5 MINUTES ▪ **COOK TIME:** 25 MINUTES

1¾   cups Swanson® Chicken Broth (Regular, Natural Goodness® *or* Certified Organic)

¾   cup *uncooked* regular long-grain white rice

1. Heat the broth in a 2-quart saucepan over medium-high heat to a boil.

2. Stir in the rice. Reduce the heat to low. Cover and cook for 20 minutes or until the rice is tender.

Florentine Simmered Rice: Add **1 teaspoon** dried Italian seasoning to broth. Add **1 cup** chopped spinach with rice. Stir in ½ **cup** grated Parmesan cheese before serving. Serve with additional cheese.

KITCHEN tip

This recipe will work with any variety of Swanson® Broth.

Moist & Savory Stuffing

MAKES 10 SERVINGS ■ **PREP TIME:** 20 MINUTES ■ **BAKE TIME:** 30 MINUTES

2½ cups Swanson® Chicken Broth (Regular, Natural Goodness® *or* Certified Organic)

Generous dash ground black pepper

2 stalks celery, coarsely chopped (about 1 cup)

1 large onion, coarsely chopped (about 1 cup)

1 package (16 ounces) Pepperidge Farm® Herb Seasoned Stuffing

1. Heat the broth, black pepper, celery and onion in a 3-quart saucepan over medium-high heat to a boil. Reduce the heat to low. Cover and cook for 5 minutes or until the vegetables are tender. Remove the saucepan from the heat. Add the stuffing and mix lightly.

2. Spoon the stuffing mixture into a greased 3-quart casserole dish. Cover the baking dish.

3. Bake at 350°F. for 30 minutes or until the stuffing is hot.

KITCHEN tip

For crunchier stuffing, bake the casserole uncovered.

Cranberry & Pecan Stuffing: Stir ½ **cup each** dried cranberries **and** chopped pecans into the stuffing mixture.

Sausage & Mushroom Stuffing: Add **1 cup** sliced mushrooms to the vegetables during cooking. Stir ½ **pound** cooked and crumbled pork sausage into the stuffing mixture.

Campbell's Easiest Prep Dishes

Spinach Ricotta Gnocchi

MAKES 6 SERVINGS ▪ **PREP TIME:** 5 MINUTES ▪ **COOK TIME:** 25 MINUTES

- 1 package (16 ounces) frozen dumpling-shaped pasta (gnocchi)
- 2 cups frozen cut leaf spinach, thawed and well drained
- 1½ cups Prego® Heart Smart Onion and Garlic Italian Sauce *or* Heart Smart Traditional Italian Sauce
- ¼ cup grated Romano cheese
- ½ cup ricotta cheese
- 1 cup shredded mozzarella cheese (about 4 ounces)

1. Prepare the gnocchi according to the package directions in a 6-quart saucepot. Add the spinach during the last 3 minutes of cooking time. Drain the gnocchi mixture well in a colander. Return the gnocchi mixture to the saucepot.

2. Stir the Italian sauce, Romano cheese and ricotta cheese in the saucepot. Cook over medium heat until the mixture is hot and bubbling, stirring occasionally. Top with the mozzarella cheese.

Campbell's Easiest Prep Dishes

Southern-Style Barbecued Chicken

MAKES 8 SERVINGS ■ **PREP TIME:** 10 MINUTES ■ **GRILL TIME:** 35 MINUTES

1   can (26 ounces) Campbell's® Condensed Tomato Soup

¼   cup honey

2   teaspoons dry mustard

1   teaspoon onion powder

8   bone-in chicken breast halves (about 4 pounds), skin removed

1. Stir the soup, honey, mustard and onion powder in a 1-quart saucepan.

2. Lightly oil the grill rack and heat the grill to medium. Grill the chicken for 20 minutes, turning the chicken over once during grilling. Brush the chicken with the soup mixture and grill for 15 minutes or until cooked through, turning and brushing often with the soup mixture.

3. Heat the remaining soup mixture to a boil and serve with the chicken.

KITCHEN

This recipe can be halved to make 4 servings. Use a **10¾-ounce can** *Campbell's® Condensed Tomato Soup, and reduce the other ingredients by half.*

Easiest Prep Dishes

Beef & Pasta

MAKES 4 SERVINGS ▪ **PREP TIME:** 5 MINUTES ▪ **COOK TIME:** 25 MINUTES

¾	pound ground beef (85% lean)
1¾	cups Swanson® Vegetable Broth (Regular *or* Certified Organic)
1	tablespoon Worcestershire sauce
½	teaspoon dried oregano leaves, crushed
½	teaspoon garlic powder
1	can (about 8 ounces) stewed tomatoes
1½	cups *uncooked* medium tube-shaped *or* corkscrew-shaped pasta

1. Cook the beef in a 10-inch skillet over medium-high heat until it's well browned, stirring often to separate the meat. Pour off any fat.

2. Stir the broth, Worcestershire, oregano, garlic and tomatoes in the skillet and heat to a boil. Stir in the pasta. Reduce the heat to low. Cover and cook for 10 minutes, stirring often. **Uncover**.

3. Cook for 5 minutes or until the pasta is tender.

15-Minute Chicken & Rice Dinner

MAKES 4 SERVINGS ▧ **PREP TIME:** 10 MINUTES ▧ **COOK TIME:** 15 MINUTES

1	tablespoon vegetable oil
4	skinless, boneless chicken breast halves (about 1 pound)
1	can (10¾ ounces) Campbell's® Condensed Cream of Chicken Soup (Regular *or* 98% Fat Free)
1½	cups water
¼	teaspoon paprika
¼	teaspoon ground black pepper
2	cups *uncooked* instant white rice*
2	cups frozen vegetable combination (broccoli, carrots, cauliflower)

For a creamier dish, decrease the rice to 1½ cups.

1. Heat the oil in a 10-inch skillet over medium-high heat. Add the chicken and cook for 10 minutes or until well browned on both sides. Remove the chicken from the skillet.

2. Stir the soup, water, paprika and black pepper in the skillet and heat to a boil. Stir in the rice and vegetables. Reduce the heat to low. Return the chicken to the skillet. Sprinkle the chicken with additional paprika and black pepper. Cover and cook for 5 minutes or until the chicken is cooked through.

KITCHEN tip

This recipe is also delicious using Campbell's® Condensed Cream of Mushroom Soup instead of the Cream of Chicken.

 Easiest Prep Dishes

New Orleans Shrimp Toss

MAKES 4 SERVINGS ▪ **PREP TIME:** 15 MINUTES ▪ **COOK TIME:** 10 MINUTES

- 1 pound large shrimp, peeled and deveined
- 2 tablespoons vegetable oil
- 2 tablespoons lemon juice
- 1 tablespoon Worcestershire sauce
- 1 teaspoon Cajun seasoning
- 1 medium onion, chopped (about ½ cup)
- 2 cloves garlic, chopped
- 1 can (10¾ ounces) Campbell's® Condensed Cream of Chicken with Herbs Soup
- ½ cup milk
- 1 teaspoon paprika
- 2 tablespoons chopped fresh chives
  Cornbread *or* biscuits

1. Stir the shrimp, **1 tablespoon** oil, lemon juice, Worcestershire and Cajun seasoning in a medium bowl.

2. Heat the remaining oil in a 10-inch skillet over medium heat. Add the onion and garlic and cook until they're tender.

3. Stir the soup, milk and paprika in the skillet. Heat to a boil. Add the shrimp mixture. Reduce the heat to low. Cover and cook for 5 minutes or until the shrimp turn pink. Garnish with the chives. Serve with cornbread.

 Easiest Prep Dishes

Quick Chicken Parmesan

MAKES 4 SERVINGS ▪ **PREP TIME:** 5 MINUTES ▪ **BAKE TIME:** 25 MINUTES

- 4 skinless, boneless chicken breast halves (about 1 pound)
- 2 cups Prego® Traditional Italian Sauce *or* Fresh Mushroom Italian Sauce
- 2 ounces shredded mozzarella cheese (about ½ cup)
- 2 tablespoons grated Parmesan cheese
- ½ of a 16-ounce package spaghetti, cooked and drained (about 4 cups)

1. Place the chicken in a 2-quart shallow baking dish. Top the chicken with the Italian sauce. Sprinkle with the mozzarella cheese and Parmesan cheese.

2. Bake at 400°F. for 25 minutes or until cooked through. Serve with the spaghetti.

Campbells Easiest Prep Dishes

Broccoli & Garlic Penne Pasta

MAKES 4 SERVINGS ▓ **PREP TIME:** 20 MINUTES ▓ **COOK TIME:** 10 MINUTES

1	cup Swanson® Chicken Broth (Regular, Natural Goodness® *or* Certified Organic)
½	teaspoon dried basil leaves, crushed
⅛	teaspoon ground black pepper
2	cloves garlic, minced
3	cups broccoli flowerets
4½	cups penne pasta, cooked and drained
1	tablespoon lemon juice
2	tablespoons grated Parmesan cheese

1. Heat the broth, basil, black pepper, garlic and broccoli in a 10-inch skillet over medium heat to a boil. Reduce the heat to low. Cover and cook until the broccoli is tender-crisp.

2. Add the pasta and lemon juice and toss to coat. Sprinkle the pasta mixture with the cheese.

Chicken Dijon with Noodles

MAKES 4 SERVINGS ■ **PREP TIME:** 5 MINUTES ■ **COOK TIME:** 25 MINUTES

2 tablespoons butter

4 skinless, boneless chicken breast halves (about 1 pound)

1 medium onion, chopped (about ½ cup)

1 can (10¾ ounces) Campbell's® Condensed Cream of Mushroom Soup (Regular *or* 98% Fat Free)

¼ cup apple juice *or* milk

1 tablespoon Dijon-style mustard

1 tablespoon chopped fresh parsley

Hot cooked noodles

1. Heat the butter in a 10-inch skillet over medium-high heat. Add the chicken and cook for 10 minutes or until it's well browned on both sides. Remove the chicken and set aside.

2. Reduce the heat to medium. Add the onion and cook until tender.

3. Stir the soup, apple juice, mustard and parsley into the skillet. Heat to a boil. Return the chicken to the skillet and reduce the heat to low. Cover and cook for 5 minutes or until the chicken is cooked through. Serve with the noodles.

KITCHEN

Cut up leftover chicken and add back to leftover sauce. Reheat chicken mixture and serve over toast topped with some chopped apple.

 Easiest Prep Dishes

Quick Chicken & Noodles

MAKES 4 SERVINGS ■ **PREP TIME:** 5 MINUTES ■ **COOK TIME:** 25 MINUTES

4	skinless, boneless chicken breast halves (about 1 pound)
½	teaspoon garlic powder
⅛	teaspoon paprika
1¾	cups Swanson® Chicken Stock
½	teaspoon dried basil leaves, crushed
¼	teaspoon ground black pepper
2	cups frozen vegetable combination (broccoli, cauliflower, carrots)
2	cups *uncooked* medium egg noodles

1. Season the chicken with the garlic powder and paprika. Cook the chicken in a 12-inch nonstick skillet over medium-high heat until it's well browned on both sides.

2. Add the stock, basil, black pepper and vegetables to the skillet and heat to a boil. Stir in the noodles. Reduce the heat to low. Cover and cook for 10 minutes or until the chicken is cooked through and the noodles are tender.

Campbell's Easiest Prep Dishes

15-Minute Herbed Chicken

MAKES 4 SERVINGS ■ **PREP TIME:** 5 MINUTES ■ **COOK TIME:** 15 MINUTES

1   tablespoon vegetable oil

4   skinless, boneless chicken breast halves (about 1 pound)

1   can (10¾ ounces) Campbell's® Condensed Cream of Chicken with Herbs Soup

½   cup milk

   Broth Simmered Rice

1. Heat the oil in a 10-inch skillet over medium-high heat. Add the chicken and cook for 10 minutes or until well browned on both sides.

2. Stir the soup and milk in the skillet and heat to a boil. Reduce the heat to low. Cover and cook for 5 minutes or until the chicken is cooked through. Serve the chicken and sauce with the *Broth Simmered Rice*.

Broth Simmered Rice: Heat **1 can** Campbell's® Condensed Chicken Broth and **1 cup** water in a 3-quart saucepan over medium-high heat to a boil. Stir in **2 cups uncooked** white rice. Cover and remove from the heat. Let stand for 5 minutes.

Campbell's Easiest Prep Dishes

Quick & Easy Dinner Nachos Supreme

MAKES 4 SERVINGS ■ **PREP TIME:** 10 MINUTES ■ **COOK TIME:** 15 MINUTES

- 1 **pound ground beef**
- 1 **package (about 1 ounce) taco seasoning mix**
- 1 **can (10¾ ounces) Campbell's® Condensed Tomato Soup**
- 1½ **cups water**
- 1½ **cups *uncooked* instant white rice**
   Pace® Chunky Salsa
   Shredded Cheddar cheese
   Shredded lettuce
   Tortilla chips

1. Cook the beef and taco seasoning in a 10-inch skillet until the beef is well browned, stirring often to separate the meat. Pour off any fat.

2. Stir the soup, water and rice in the skillet and heat to a boil. Reduce the heat to low. Cover and cook for 5 minutes or until the rice is tender.

3. Top with the salsa, cheese and lettuce. Serve with the tortilla chips for dipping.

Tasty 2-Step Chicken

MAKES 4 SERVINGS ■ **PREP TIME:** 5 MINUTES ■ **COOK TIME:** 20 MINUTES

- 1 tablespoon vegetable oil
- 4 skinless, boneless chicken breast halves (about 1 pound)
- 1 can (10¾ ounces) Campbell's® Condensed Cream of Mushroom Soup (Regular, 98% Fat Free *or* Healthy Request®)
- ½ cup water

1. Heat the oil in a 10-inch skillet over medium-high heat. Add the chicken and cook for 10 minutes or until well browned on both sides. Remove the chicken from the skillet.

2. Stir the soup and water in the skillet and heat to a boil. Return the chicken to the skillet. Reduce the heat to low. Cover and cook for 5 minutes or until the chicken is cooked through.

KITCHEN tip *This recipe is also delicious with Campbell's® Condensed Cream of Mushroom with Roasted Garlic Soup **or** Cream of Chicken with Herbs Soup.*

Campbell's Easiest Prep Dishes

Skillet Chicken & Rice

MAKES 4 SERVINGS ■ **PREP TIME:** 5 MINUTES ■ **COOK TIME:** 35 MINUTES

1	pound skinless, boneless chicken breasts, cut into cubes
1¾	cups Swanson® Chicken Stock
½	teaspoon dried basil leaves, crushed
½	teaspoon garlic powder
¾	cup *uncooked* regular long-grain white rice
1	package (16 ounces) frozen vegetable combination (broccoli, cauliflower, carrots)

1. Cook the chicken in a 10-inch nonstick skillet over medium-high heat until it's well browned, stirring often. Remove the chicken from the skillet.

2. Stir in the stock, basil and garlic powder and heat to a boil. Stir in the rice. Reduce the heat to low. Cover and cook for 5 minutes.

3. Stir in the vegetables. Return the chicken to the skillet. Cover and cook for 15 minutes or until the chicken is cooked through and the rice is tender.

  Easiest Prep Dishes

Ultra Creamy Mashed Potatoes

MAKES 6 SERVINGS ▪ **PREP TIME:** 15 MINUTES ▪ **COOK TIME:** 20 MINUTES

3½ cups Swanson® Chicken Broth (Regular, Natural Goodness® *or* Certified Organic)

5 large potatoes, cut into 1-inch pieces (about 7½ cups)

½ cup light cream

2 tablespoons butter

Generous dash ground black pepper

1 can (14½ ounces) Campbell's® Turkey Gravy

1. Heat the broth and potatoes in a 3-quart saucepan over medium-high heat to a boil.

2. Reduce the heat to medium. Cover and cook for 10 minutes or until the potatoes are tender. Drain, reserving the broth.

3. Mash the potatoes with ¼ **cup** broth, cream, butter and black pepper. Add additional broth, if needed, until desired consistency. Serve with the gravy.

Ultimate Mashed Potatoes: Stir ½ **cup** sour cream, **3** slices bacon, cooked and crumbled (reserve some for garnish), and ¼ **cup** chopped fresh chives into the hot mashed potatoes. Sprinkle with the reserved bacon.

Quick Spaghetti & Meatballs

MAKES 6 SERVINGS ▓ **PREP TIME:** 5 MINUTES ▓ **COOK TIME:** 25 MINUTES

  1   jar (45 ounces) Prego® Flavored with Meat Italian Sauce

16   frozen meatballs (1 ounce *each*)

  1   package (16 ounces) spaghetti, cooked and drained (about 8 cups)

      Grated Parmesan cheese

1. Stir the Italian sauce and meatballs in 3-quart saucepan and heat to a boil over medium heat. Reduce the heat to low. Cover and cook for 20 minutes or until the meatballs are heated through, stirring occasionally.

2. Serve the sauce and meatballs over the spaghetti. Sprinkle with the cheese.

Asian Chicken & Rice

MAKES 4 SERVINGS ▪ **PREP TIME:** 5 MINUTES ▪ **COOK TIME:** 20 MINUTES

1	tablespoon vegetable oil
4	skinless, boneless chicken breast halves (about 1 pound)
1	can (10¾ ounces) Campbell's® Condensed Golden Mushroom Soup
1½	cups water
1	package (1.25 ounces) teriyaki seasoning mix
1	bag (16 ounces) frozen stir-fry vegetables
1½	cups *uncooked* instant white rice

1. Heat the oil in a 10-inch skillet over medium-high heat. Add the chicken and cook until well browned on both sides. Remove the chicken from the skillet.

2. Stir the soup, water, seasoning mix and vegetables in the skillet and heat to a boil. Stir in the rice. Return the chicken to the pan. Reduce the heat to low. Cover and cook for 5 minutes or until the chicken is cooked through and the rice is tender.

Polenta Sausage Bake

MAKES 8 SERVINGS ▪ **PREP TIME:** 20 MINUTES ▪ **BAKE TIME:** 25 MINUTES

- 24 ounces prepared polenta, cut into ½-inch-thick slices
- ¼ cup grated Parmesan cheese
- 1 pound sweet *or* hot Italian pork sausage, casing removed
- 1 large zucchini, cut in half lengthwise and sliced (about 2 cups)
- 2 cups Prego® Traditional Italian Sauce *or* Roasted Garlic & Herb Italian Sauce
- 6 ounces shredded fontina *or* mozzarella cheese (about 1½ cups)

1. Heat the oven to 400°F. Arrange the polenta slices to cover the bottom of a 3-quart shallow baking dish, trimming the slices as needed to fit. Sprinkle with the Parmesan cheese.

2. Cook the sausage in a 12-inch skillet over medium-high heat until it's well browned, stirring often to separate the meat. Remove the sausage from the skillet. Pour off any fat.

3. Add the zucchini to the skillet and cook for 3 minutes or until it's tender. Stir in the Italian sauce and heat to a boil. Return the sausage to the skillet. Cook until the mixture is hot and bubbling. Spoon the sausage mixture over the polenta. Top with the fontina cheese.

4. Bake for 25 minutes or until hot and the cheese is melted.

One-Dish Wonders

Citrus Chicken and Rice
(recipe page 104)

Citrus Chicken and Rice

MAKES 4 SERVINGS ▪ **PREP TIME:** 5 MINUTES ▪ **COOK TIME:** 35 MINUTES

4	skinless, boneless chicken breasts halves (about 1 pound)
1¾	cups Swanson® Chicken Stock
¾	cup orange juice
1	medium onion, chopped (about ½ cup)
1	cup *uncooked* regular long-grain white rice
3	tablespoons chopped fresh parsley

1. Cook the chicken in a 10-inch nonstick skillet over medium-high heat for 10 minutes or until it's well browned on both sides. Remove the chicken from the skillet.

2. Stir the stock, orange juice, onion and rice in the skillet and heat to a boil. Reduce the heat to low. Cover and cook for 10 minutes.

3. Return the chicken to the skillet. Cover and cook for 10 minutes or until the chicken is cooked through and the rice is tender. Stir in the parsley.

KITCHEN tip *For a special touch, cook orange slices in a nonstick skillet over medium-high heat until they're lightly browned. Serve over the chicken.*

Campbell's One-Dish Wonders

Ham and Asparagus Strata

MAKES 8 SERVINGS ■ **PREP TIME:** 15 MINUTES ■ **BAKE TIME:** 45 MINUTES
STAND TIME: 5 MINUTES

4	cups Pepperidge Farm® Cubed Country Style Stuffing
2	cups shredded Swiss cheese (about 8 ounces)
1½	cups cooked cut asparagus
1½	cups cubed cooked ham
1	can (10¾ ounces) Campbell's® Condensed Cream of Asparagus Soup **or** Campbell's® Condensed Cream of Mushroom Soup
2	cups milk
5	eggs
1	tablespoon Dijon-style mustard

1. Heat the oven to 350°F. Stir the stuffing, cheese, asparagus and ham in a greased 3-quart shallow baking dish.

2. Beat the soup, milk, eggs and mustard in a medium bowl with a fork or whisk. Pour over the stuffing mixture. Stir and press the stuffing mixture into the milk mixture to coat.

3. Bake for 45 minutes or until a knife inserted in the center comes out clean. Let stand for 5 minutes.

KITCHEN tip

*For 1½ **cups** cooked cut asparagus, use ¾ **pound** fresh asparagus, trimmed and cut into 1-inch pieces **or 1 package** (about 10 ounces) frozen asparagus spears, thawed, drained and cut into 1-inch pieces.*

Three Cheese Baked Ziti with Spinach

MAKES 6 SERVINGS ▪ **PREP TIME:** 15 MINUTES ▪ **BAKE TIME:** 30 MINUTES

- 1   package (16 ounces) *uncooked* medium tube-shaped pasta (ziti)
- 1   bag (6 ounces) baby spinach, washed (about 4 cups)
- 1   jar (1 pound 9 ounces) Prego® Marinara Italian Sauce
- 1   cup ricotta cheese
- 4   ounces shredded mozzarella cheese (about 1 cup)
- ¾   cup grated Parmesan cheese
- ½   teaspoon garlic powder
- ¼   teaspoon ground black pepper

1. Prepare the pasta according to the package directions. Add the spinach during the last minute of the cooking time. Drain the pasta and spinach well in a colander. Return them to the saucepot.

2. Stir the Italian sauce, ricotta, ½ **cup** of the mozzarella cheese, ½ **cup** of the Parmesan cheese, garlic powder and black pepper into the pasta mixture. Spoon the pasta mixture into a 13×9×2-inch shallow baking dish. Sprinkle with the remaining mozzarella and Parmesan cheeses.

3. Bake at 350°F. for 30 minutes or it's until hot and bubbling.

Campbell's   One-Dish Wonders

Mushroom-Smothered Beef Burgers

MAKES 4 SERVINGS ■ **PREP TIME:** 15 MINUTES ■ **COOK TIME:** 25 MINUTES

1	can (10¾ ounces) Campbell's® Condensed Cream of Mushroom Soup (Regular *or* 98% Fat Free)
1	pound ground beef
⅓	cup Italian-seasoned dry bread crumbs
1	small onion, finely chopped (about ¼ cup)
1	egg, beaten
1	tablespoon vegetable oil
1	tablespoon Worcestershire sauce
2	tablespoons water
1½	cups sliced mushrooms (about 4 ounces)

1. Thoroughly mix ¼ **cup** soup, beef, bread crumbs, onion and egg in a large bowl. Shape the beef mixture firmly into **4** (½-inch-thick) burgers.

2. Heat the oil in a 10-inch skillet over medium-high heat. Add the burgers and cook until they're well browned on both sides. Pour off any fat.

3. Add the remaining soup, Worcestershire, water and mushrooms to the skillet and heat to a boil. Reduce the heat to low. Cover and cook for 10 minutes or until the burgers are cooked through.

KITCHEN

You can substitute ground turkey for the ground beef in this recipe.

One-Dish Wonders

Pork Chop Skillet Dinner

MAKES 4 SERVINGS ■ **PREP TIME:** 10 MINUTES ■ **COOK TIME:** 40 MINUTES

1	tablespoon olive oil
4	bone-in pork chops, ¾-inch thick *each*
1	medium onion, chopped (about ½ cup)
1	cup *uncooked* regular long-grain white rice
1¼	cups Swanson® Chicken Stock
1	cup orange juice
3	tablespoons chopped fresh parsley
¼	teaspoon ground black pepper
4	orange slices

1. Heat the oil in a 12-inch skillet over medium-high heat. Add the pork and cook until it's well browned on both sides.

2. Add the onion and rice to the skillet. Cook until the rice is lightly browned.

3. Stir in the stock, orange juice, **2 tablespoons** parsley and black pepper and heat to a boil. Reduce the heat to low. Cover and cook for 20 minutes or until the pork is cooked through and the rice is tender. Top with the orange slices and sprinkle with the remaining parsley.

Campbell's One-Dish Wonders

Balsamic Beef with Mushrooms

MAKES 6 SERVINGS ▪ **PREP TIME:** 15 MINUTES ▪ **COOK TIME:** 7 HOURS

Vegetable cooking spray

1 boneless beef chuck roast, 1-inch thick (about 2 pounds)

2⅔ cups Prego® Traditional Italian Sauce

⅓ cup balsamic vinegar

2 packages (8 ounces *each*) sliced mushrooms (about 6 cups)

1 slice bacon, cooked and crumbled

Hot cooked egg noodles

1. Spray a 10-inch skillet with the cooking spray and heat over medium-high heat for 1 minute. Add the beef and cook until it's well browned on both sides.

2. Stir the Italian sauce, vinegar, mushrooms and bacon in a 5-quart slow cooker. Add the beef and turn to coat.

3. Cover and cook on LOW for 7 to 8 hours* or until the beef is fork-tender. Serve with the egg noodles.

Or on HIGH for 4 to 5 hours.

  One-Dish Wonders

Broccoli Fish Bake

MAKES 4 SERVINGS ▪ **PREP TIME:** 15 MINUTES ▪ **BAKE TIME:** 20 MINUTES

- **1** package (about 10 ounces) frozen broccoli spears, cooked and drained
- **4** fresh *or* thawed frozen firm white fish fillets (cod, haddock *or* halibut) (about 1 pound)
- **1** can (10¾ ounces) Campbell's® Condensed Cream of Broccoli Soup
- **⅓** cup milk
- **¼** cup shredded Cheddar cheese
- **2** tablespoons dry bread crumbs
- **1** teaspoon butter, melted
- **⅛** teaspoon paprika

1. Place the broccoli into a 2-quart shallow baking dish. Top with the fish. Stir the soup and milk in a small bowl. Pour the soup mixture over the fish. Sprinkle with the cheese.

2. Stir the bread crumbs, butter and paprika in a small bowl. Sprinkle the crumb mixture over all.

3. Bake at 450°F. for 20 minutes or until the fish flakes easily when tested with a fork.

KITCHEN tip *You can substitute **1 pound** fresh broccoli spears, cooked and drained, for the frozen.*

Baked Chicken & Cheese Risotto

MAKES 4 SERVINGS ▪ **PREP TIME:** 10 MINUTES

BAKE TIME: 45 MINUTES ▪ **STAND TIME:** 5 MINUTES

1	can (10¾ ounces) Campbell's® Condensed Cream of Mushroom Soup (Regular *or* 98% Fat Free)
1¼	cups water
½	cup milk
¼	cup shredded part-skim mozzarella cheese
3	tablespoons grated Parmesan cheese
1½	cups frozen mixed vegetables
2	skinless, boneless chicken breast halves (about ½ pound), cut into cubes
¾	cup *uncooked* Arborio *or* regular long-grain white rice

1. Stir the soup, water, milk, mozzarella cheese, Parmesan cheese, vegetables, chicken and rice in a 3-quart shallow baking dish. Cover the baking dish.

2. Bake at 400°F. for 35 minutes. Stir the rice mixture. Cover the baking dish.

3. Bake for 10 minutes or until the chicken is cooked through and the rice is tender. Let stand, covered, for 5 minutes.

Campbell's One-Dish Wonders

Mediterranean Chicken & Rice Bake

MAKES 6 SERVINGS ■ **PREP TIME:** 10 MINUTES ■ **BAKE TIME:** 50 MINUTES

2	cups Swanson® Chicken Stock
¼	cup chopped fresh parsley
1	can (2.25 ounces) sliced pitted ripe olives
1	tablespoon fresh lemon juice
¼	teaspoon ground black pepper
1	can (about 14.5 ounces) stewed tomatoes
1¼	cups *uncooked* regular long-grain white rice
6	skinless, boneless chicken breast halves (about 1½ pounds)
1	teaspoon garlic powder
	Paprika

1. Stir the stock, parsley, olives, lemon juice, black pepper, tomatoes and rice in a 13×9×2-inch baking dish. Cover the dish.

2. Bake at 375°F. for 20 minutes.

3. Place the chicken onto the rice mixture. Sprinkle the chicken with the garlic powder and paprika. Cover the dish.

4. Bake for 30 minutes or until the chicken is cooked through and the rice is tender.

Braised Short Ribs with Red Wine Tomato Sauce

MAKES 8 SERVINGS ▪ **PREP TIME:** 10 MINUTES ▪ **COOK TIME:** 7 HOURS

4 pounds beef short ribs, cut into serving-sized pieces

2⅔ cups Prego® Fresh Mushroom Italian Sauce

1 cup dry red wine

1 bag fresh *or* frozen whole baby carrots

1 large onion, chopped (about 1 cup)

Hot cooked rice

1. Season the ribs as desired.

2. Stir the Italian sauce, wine, carrots and onion in a 3½-quart slow cooker. Add the ribs and turn to coat.

3. Cover and cook on LOW for 7 to 8 hours* or until the ribs are fork-tender. Serve with the rice.

Or on HIGH for 4 to 5 hours.

Chicken Noodle Casserole

MAKES 4 SERVINGS ▓ **PREP TIME:** 10 MINUTES ▓ **BAKE TIME:** 25 MINUTES

1	can (10¾ ounces) Campbell's® Condensed Cream of Mushroom Soup (Regular *or* 98% Fat Free)
½	cup milk
2	tablespoons butter, melted
¼	teaspoon ground black pepper
1	cup frozen broccoli flowerets, thawed
2	cups shredded cooked chicken
2	cups hot cooked medium egg noodles
½	cup grated Parmesan cheese

1. Stir soup, milk, butter, black pepper, broccoli, chicken and noodles in a 2-quart casserole.

2. Bake at 400°F. for 20 minutes or until hot. Stir.

3. Sprinkle with the cheese. Bake for 5 minutes more.

One-Dish Chicken & Stuffing Bake

MAKES 6 SERVINGS ▪ **PREP TIME:** 15 MINUTES ▪ **BAKE TIME:** 30 MINUTES

- 4 cups Pepperidge Farm® Herb Seasoned Stuffing
- 6 skinless, boneless chicken breast halves (about 1½ pounds)
  Paprika
- 1 can (10¾ ounces) Campbell's® Condensed Cream of Mushroom Soup (Regular *or* 98% Fat Free)
- ⅓ cup milk
- 1 tablespoon chopped fresh parsley *or* 1 teaspoon dried parsley flakes

1. Heat the oven to 400°F. Prepare the stuffing according to the package directions.

2. Spoon the stuffing across the center of a 3-quart shallow baking dish. Place the chicken on either side of the stuffing. Sprinkle the chicken with the paprika.

3. Stir the soup, milk and parsley in a small bowl. Pour the soup mixture over the chicken. Cover the baking dish.

4. Bake for 30 minutes or until the chicken is cooked through.

KITCHEN

Any variety of Pepperidge Farm® Stuffing will work in this recipe.

Black Bean, Corn and Turkey Chili

MAKES 6 SERVINGS ▪ **PREP TIME:** 15 MINUTES ▪ **COOK TIME:** 40 MINUTES

- 1 tablespoon vegetable oil
- 1 pound ground turkey
- 1 large onion, chopped (about 1 cup)
- 2 tablespoons chili powder
- 1 teaspoon ground cumin
- 1 teaspoon dried oregano leaves, crushed
- ½ teaspoon ground black pepper
- ¼ teaspoon garlic powder *or* 2 cloves garlic, minced
- 1¾ cups Swanson® Chicken Stock
- 1 cup Pace® Picante Sauce
- 1 tablespoon sugar
- 1 can (about 15 ounces) black beans, rinsed and drained
- 1 can (about 16 ounces) whole kernel corn, drained

1. Heat the oil in a 4-quart saucepan over medium-high heat. Add the turkey, onion, chili powder, cumin, oregano, black pepper and garlic powder. Cook until the turkey is well browned, stirring often to separate the meat.

2. Stir the stock, picante sauce, sugar, beans and corn in the saucepan and heat to a boil. Reduce the heat to low. Cover and cook for 30 minutes or until the mixture is hot and bubbling.

Pork Chops & Stuffing Bake

MAKES 6 SERVINGS ▪ **PREP TIME:** 10 MINUTES ▪ **BAKE TIME:** 30 MINUTES

4   cups Pepperidge Farm® Corn Bread Stuffing

1¼   cups water

¼   cup (½ stick) butter

6   boneless pork chops, ¾-inch thick (about 1½ pounds)

1   can (10¾ ounces) Campbell's® Condensed Cream of Celery Soup
     (Regular *or* 98% Fat Free)

⅓   cup milk

½   cup shredded Cheddar cheese

1. Prepare the stuffing with the water and butter according to the package directions.

2. Spoon the stuffing across the center of a 3-quart shallow baking dish. Place the pork on each side of the stuffing.

3. Stir the soup and milk in a small bowl. Pour the soup mixture over the pork. Cover the baking dish.

4. Bake at 400°F. for 30 minutes or until the pork is cooked through. Sprinkle with the cheese.

Campbell's One-Dish Wonders

Chicken Broccoli Divan

MAKES 4 SERVINGS ▪ **PREP TIME:** 15 MINUTES ▪ **BAKE TIME:** 20 MINUTES

- **1 pound fresh broccoli, cut into spears *or* 1 package (10 ounces) frozen broccoli spears, cooked and drained**
- **1 can (12.5 ounces) Swanson® Premium White Chunk Chicken Breast in Water, drained**
- **1 can (10¾ ounces) Campbell's® Condensed Broccoli Cheese Soup (Regular *or* 98% Fat Free)**
- **⅓ cup milk**
- **½ cup shredded Cheddar cheese**
- **2 tablespoons dry bread crumbs**
- **1 tablespoon butter, melted**

1. Place the broccoli and chicken into a 9-inch pie plate. Stir the soup and milk in a small bowl. Pour the soup mixture over the broccoli and chicken.

2. Sprinkle the cheese over the soup mixture. Stir the bread crumbs and butter in a small bowl. Sprinkle the bread crumb mixture over the cheese.

KITCHEN tip

For cornflake topping, substitute cornflakes for the bread crumbs and omit the butter.

3. Bake at 450°F. for 20 minutes or until the cheese is melted and the bread crumb mixture is golden brown.

Chicken Mushroom Risotto

MAKES 4 SERVINGS ■ **PREP TIME:** 15 MINUTES ■ **COOK TIME:** 35 MINUTES

3 skinless, boneless chicken breast halves (about ¾ pound), cut into cubes

1 small onion, finely chopped (about ¼ cup)

1 small carrot, chopped (about ¼ cup)

1 cup *uncooked* regular long-grain white rice

1 can (10¾ ounces) Campbell's® Healthy Request® Condensed Cream of Mushroom Soup

1¾ cups Swanson® Chicken Stock

⅛ teaspoon ground black pepper

½ cup frozen peas

1. Cook the chicken in a 10-inch nonstick skillet over medium-high heat until well browned, stirring often. Remove the chicken from the skillet.

2. Stir the onion, carrot and rice in the skillet and cook and stir until the rice is browned.

3. Stir in the soup, stock and black pepper and heat to a boil. Reduce the heat to low. Cover and cook for 15 minutes.

4. Stir in the peas. Return the chicken to the skillet. Cover and cook for 5 minutes or until the chicken is cooked through and the rice is tender.

Campbell's One-Dish Wonders

Cheesy Chicken & Rice Casserole

MAKES 4 SERVINGS ▪ **PREP TIME:** 15 MINUTES ▪ **BAKE TIME:** 50 MINUTES
STAND TIME: 10 MINUTES

1	can (10¾ ounces) Campbell's® Condensed Cream of Chicken Soup (Regular, 98% Fat Free *or* Healthy Request®)
1⅓	cups water
¾	cup *uncooked* regular long-grain white rice
½	teaspoon onion powder
¼	teaspoon ground black pepper
2	cups frozen mixed vegetables
4	skinless, boneless chicken breast halves (about 1 pound)
½	cup shredded Cheddar cheese

1. Heat the oven to 375°F. Stir the soup, water, rice, onion powder, black pepper and vegetables in a 2-quart shallow baking dish.

2. Top with the chicken. Cover the baking dish.

3. Bake for 50 minutes or until the chicken is cooked through and the rice is tender. Top with the cheese. Let the casserole stand for 10 minutes. Stir the rice before serving.

Lower Fat: Use Campbell's® 98% Fat Free Cream of Chicken Soup instead of regular soup and use low-fat cheese instead of regular cheese.

Mexican: In place of the onion powder and black pepper use **1 teaspoon** chili powder. Substitute Mexican cheese blend for the Cheddar.

Italian: In place of the onion powder and black pepper use **1 teaspoon** Italian seasoning, crushed. Substitute ⅓ **cup** shredded Parmesan for the Cheddar.

Easy Chicken & Biscuits

MAKES 4 SERVINGS ■ **PREP TIME:** 10 MINUTES ■ **BAKE TIME:** 35 MINUTES

- 1 can (10¾ ounces) Campbell's® Condensed Cream of Broccoli Soup (Regular *or* 98% Fat Free)
- 1 can (10¾ ounces) Campbell's® Condensed Cream of Potato Soup
- ⅔ cup milk
- ½ teaspoon poultry seasoning
- ⅛ teaspoon ground black pepper
- 2 cups frozen mixed vegetables
- 2 cups cubed cooked chicken *or* turkey
- 1 package (7.5 ounces) refrigerated biscuits

1. Stir the soups, milk, poultry seasoning, black pepper, vegetables and chicken in a 2-quart shallow baking dish.

2. Bake at 400°F. for 20 minutes or until the chicken mixture is hot and bubbling. Stir the chicken mixture. Top with the biscuits.

3. Bake for 15 minutes or until the biscuits are golden brown.

KITCHEN tip Substitute Campbell's® Condensed Cream of Celery Soup for the Cream of Broccoli.

Zesty Turkey & Rice

MAKES 4 SERVINGS ■ **PREP TIME:** 5 MINUTES ■ **COOK TIME:** 30 MINUTES

2	cups Swanson® Chicken Stock
1	teaspoon dried basil leaves, crushed
¼	teaspoon garlic powder
¼	teaspoon hot pepper sauce
1	can (about 14.5 ounces) stewed tomatoes
¾	cup *uncooked* regular long-grain white rice
1	cup frozen peas
2	cups cubed cooked turkey *or* chicken

1. Heat the stock, basil, garlic powder, hot pepper sauce and tomatoes in a 2½-quart saucepan over medium heat to a boil. Stir in the rice. Reduce the heat to low. Cover and cook for 20 minutes.

2. Stir in the peas and turkey. Cover and cook for 5 minutes or until the rice is done.

Campbell's One-Dish Wonders

Easy One-Pot Spaghetti & Clams

MAKES 8 SERVINGS ■ **PREP TIME:** 5 MINUTES ■ **COOK TIME:** 20 MINUTES

3	tablespoons olive oil
3	cloves garlic, minced
¼	teaspoon crushed red pepper flakes
8	cups Swanson® Chicken Stock
1	can (6.5 ounces) chopped clams, undrained
1	package (1 pound) *uncooked* thin spaghetti
1	can (10 ounces) whole baby clams, undrained
16	littleneck clams, scrubbed
⅓	cup chopped fresh parsley

1. Heat the oil in a 4-quart saucepan over medium heat. Add the garlic and red pepper. Cook for 1 minute. Add the stock and chopped clams. Heat to a boil.

2. Add the spaghetti. Cook for about 9 minutes or until the stock is absorbed. Add the canned and fresh clams. Cook for 2 minutes or until the fresh clams open. Toss with the parsley.

KITCHEN tip

If using fresh clams, the shells should be tightly closed. If the shells are open, tap them slightly and if they don't close shut, then the clam is no longer alive and should be discarded. Also, after cooking discard any clams that do not open.

Herb Roasted Chicken & Vegetables

MAKES 4 SERVINGS ▪ **PREP TIME:** 10 MINUTES ▪ **BAKE TIME:** 50 MINUTES

- 1 can (10¾ ounces) Campbell's® Condensed Cream of Mushroom Soup (Regular *or* 98% Fat Free)
- ⅓ cup water
- 2 teaspoons dried oregano leaves, crushed
- 4 medium potatoes, cut into quarters (about 1¼ pounds)
- 2 cups fresh *or* frozen baby carrots
- 4 bone-in chicken breast halves (about 2 pounds)
- ½ teaspoon paprika

1. Stir the soup, water, **1 teaspoon** of the oregano, potatoes and carrots in a roasting pan.

2. Top with the chicken. Sprinkle with the remaining oregano and paprika.

3. Bake at 400°F. for 50 minutes or until the chicken is cooked through. Stir the vegetable mixture before serving.

KITCHEN *Substitute white wine for the water.*

 One-Dish Wonders

Rosemary Chicken & Roasted Vegetables

MAKES 4 SERVINGS ■ **PREP TIME:** 15 MINUTES

COOK TIME: 1 HOUR 15 MINUTES

1	(3-pound) whole broiler-fryer chicken
1	tablespoon butter, melted
4	medium red potatoes, cut into quarters
2	cups fresh *or* frozen whole baby carrots
2	stalks celery, cut into 2-inch pieces (about 1½ cups)
12	small white onions, peeled
1½	teaspoons chopped fresh rosemary leaves *or* ½ teaspoon dried rosemary leaves, crushed
1	cup Swanson® Chicken Stock
½	cup orange juice

1. Brush the chicken with the butter. Place the chicken and vegetables into a 17×11-inch roasting pan. Season with the rosemary. Stir the stock and orange juice in a small bowl and pour **half** the stock mixture over the chicken and vegetables.

2. Roast at 375°F. for 45 minutes.

3. Stir the vegetables. Add the remaining stock mixture to the pan. Roast for 30 minutes or until the chicken is cooked through.

KITCHEN

To quickly peel the onions, place them into a medium bowl. Pour boiling water over the onions to cover. Let stand for 5 minutes. Drain and slip off the skins.

One-Dish Wonders

White Chicken Chili

MAKES 5 SERVINGS ■ **PREP TIME:** 10 MINUTES ■ **COOK TIME:** 30 MINUTES

1 tablespoon vegetable oil

4 skinless, boneless chicken breast halves (about 1 pound), cut into cubes

1 tablespoon chili powder

1 can (10¾ ounces) Campbell's® Condensed Cream of Chicken Soup (Regular *or* 98% Fat Free)

2 cups water

1 envelope (about 1 ounce) dry onion soup and recipe mix

2 cans (about 15 ounces *each*) white kidney beans (cannellini), rinsed and drained

Shredded Cheddar cheese

Sliced green onion

1. Heat the oil in a 3-quart saucepan over medium-high heat. Add the chicken and chili powder and cook until the chicken is well browned, stirring often.

2. Stir the soup, water and soup mix in the saucepan and heat to a boil. Reduce the heat to low. Cover and cook for 10 minutes.

3. Stir in the beans and cook until the mixture is hot and bubbling. Serve with the cheese and onions.

One-Dish Chicken & Rice Bake

MAKES 4 SERVINGS ▪ **PREP TIME:** 5 MINUTES ▪ **BAKE TIME:** 45 MINUTES

1	can (10¾ ounces) Campbell's® Condensed Cream of Mushroom Soup (Regular *or* 98% Fat Free)
1	cup water*
¾	cup *uncooked* regular long-grain white rice
¼	teaspoon paprika
¼	teaspoon ground black pepper
4	skinless, boneless chicken breast halves (about 1 pound)

For creamier rice, increase the water to 1⅓ cups.

1. Stir the soup, water, rice, paprika and black pepper in a 2-quart shallow baking dish. Top with the chicken. Season with additional paprika and black pepper. Cover the baking dish.

2. Bake at 375°F. for 45 minutes or until the chicken is cooked through and the rice is tender.

Scalloped Potato-Onion Bake

MAKES 6 SERVINGS ▪ **PREP TIME:** 10 MINUTES
BAKE TIME: 1 HOUR 15 MINUTES

1   can (10¾ ounces) Campbell's® Condensed Cream of Celery Soup (Regular *or* 98% Fat Free)

½   cup milk

Dash ground black pepper

4   medium potatoes (about 1¼ pounds), thinly sliced

1   small onion, thinly sliced (about ¼ cup)

1   tablespoon butter, cut into small pieces

Paprika

1. Stir the soup, milk and black pepper in a small bowl. Layer **half** the potatoes, onion and soup mixture in a 1½-quart casserole. Repeat the layers. Dot the top with the butter. Sprinkle with the paprika. Cover the baking dish.

2. Bake at 400°F. for 1 hour. Uncover the dish and bake for 15 minutes or until the potatoes are tender.

Campbell's One-Dish Wonders

Roasted Asparagus with Lemon & Goat Cheese

MAKES 6 SERVINGS ▓ **PREP TIME:** 10 MINUTES ▓ **COOK TIME:** 20 MINUTES

Vegetable cooking spray

2 pounds asparagus, trimmed

1 tablespoon olive oil

Freshly ground black pepper

½ cup Swanson® Vegetable Broth

3 ounces soft goat cheese, crumbled

1 tablespoon lemon juice

1 teaspoon grated lemon peel

1. Heat the oven to 425°F. Spray a 17×11-inch roasting pan or shallow baking sheet with the cooking spray.

2. Stir the asparagus and oil in the pan. Season with the black pepper. Pour in the broth.

3. Roast the asparagus for 20 minutes or until it's tender, stirring once during cooking. Top with the cheese, lemon juice and lemon peel.

Campbell's One-Dish Wonders

Fun Food
for Kids

*Baked Macaroni and Cheese
(recipe page 150)*

Baked Macaroni and Cheese

MAKES 4 SERVINGS ▪ **PREP TIME:** 20 MINUTES ▪ **BAKE TIME:** 20 MINUTES

1	can (10¾ ounces) Campbell's® Condensed Cheddar Cheese Soup
½	soup can milk
⅛	teaspoon ground black pepper
2	cups corkscrew-shaped pasta (rotini) *or* shell-shaped pasta
1	tablespoon dry bread crumbs
2	teaspoons butter, melted

1. Stir the soup, milk, black pepper and pasta in a 1-quart baking dish.

2. Stir the bread crumbs and butter in a small bowl. Sprinkle the bread crumb mixture over the pasta mixture.

3. Bake at 400°F. for 20 minutes or until the pasta mixture is hot and bubbling.

Broccoli Cheese Skillet Potatoes

MAKES 4 SERVINGS ▪ **PREP TIME:** 15 MINUTES ▪ **COOK TIME:** 10 MINUTES

  2 tablespoons butter

  1 small onion, sliced (about ¼ cup)

  1 can (10¾ ounces) Campbell's® Condensed Broccoli Cheese Soup
     (Regular *or* 98% Fat Free)

  ⅓ cup milk

  ⅛ teaspoon ground black pepper

  4 medium potatoes (about 1¼ pounds), cooked and sliced
     ¼-inch thick

     Chopped fresh parsley for garnish

1. Heat the butter in a 10-inch skillet over medium heat. Add the onion and cook until it's tender.

2. Stir the soup, milk, black pepper and potatoes in the skillet and heat through. Sprinkle with parsley.

KITCHEN tip

*You can substitute **2 cans** (about 16 ounces **each**) whole white potatoes, rinsed, drained and sliced for the medium potatoes.*

Chicken & Tortellini Stew

MAKES 6 SERVINGS ■ **PREP TIME:** 15 MINUTES ■ **COOK TIME:** 35 MINUTES

- 1 tablespoon cornstarch
- 1 tablespoon water
- 2 tablespoons vegetable oil
- 3 skinless, boneless chicken breast halves (about ¾ pound), cut into cubes
- 1 cup frozen sliced carrots
- 1 cup frozen cut green beans
- ¾ cup chopped onion
- 6 cups Swanson® Chicken Stock
- 1 cup *uncooked* dry cheese-filled tortellini
- 2 tablespoons chopped fresh parsley

1. Stir the cornstarch and water in a small bowl until the mixture is smooth.

2. Heat **1 tablespoon** oil in a 6-quart saucepot over medium-high heat. Add the chicken and cook until it's well browned, stirring often. Remove the chicken from the saucepot.

3. Heat the remaining oil in the saucepot over medium heat. Add the carrots, beans and onion and cook until they're tender-crisp.

4. Stir in the stock and heat to a boil. Add the tortellini and parsley, if desired. Cook for 10 minutes or until the tortellini is tender. Return the chicken to the saucepot and cook until the chicken is cooked through.

5. Stir in the cornstarch mixture. Cook and stir until the mixture boils and thickens.

 Fun Food for Kids

Easy Chicken Pot Pie

MAKES 4 SERVINGS ■ **PREP TIME:** 10 MINUTES ■ **BAKE TIME:** 30 MINUTES

- 1 can (10¾ ounces) Campbell's® Condensed Cream of Chicken Soup (Regular *or* 98% Fat Free)
- 1 package (9 ounces) frozen mixed vegetables, thawed
- 1 cup cubed cooked chicken *or* turkey
- ½ cup milk
- 1 egg
- 1 cup all-purpose baking mix

1. Heat the oven to 400°F. Stir the soup, vegetables and chicken in a 9-inch pie plate.

2. Stir the milk, egg and baking mix in a small bowl. Spread the batter over the chicken mixture.

3. Bake for 30 minutes or until the topping is golden brown.

KITCHEN tip

You can easily substitute Campbell's® Condensed Cream of Chicken with Herbs Soup for the Cream of Chicken.

Substitute reduced-fat all-purpose baking mix for the regular baking mix.

Campbell's Fun Food for Kids

Tuna & Pasta Cheddar Melt

MAKES 4 SERVINGS ■ **PREP TIME:** 10 MINUTES ■ **COOK TIME:** 15 MINUTES

1   can (10½ ounces) Campbell's® Condensed Chicken Broth

1   soup can water

3   cups *uncooked* corkscrew-shaped pasta (rotini)

1   can (10¾ ounces) Campbell's® Condensed Cream of Mushroom Soup (Regular *or* 98% Fat Free)

1   cup milk

1   can (about 6 ounces) tuna, drained and flaked

1   cup shredded Cheddar cheese (about 4 ounces)

2   tablespoons Italian-seasoned dry bread crumbs

2   teaspoons butter, melted

1. Heat the broth and water in a 12-inch skillet over medium-high heat to a boil. Stir in the pasta. Reduce the heat to medium. Cook until the pasta is tender, stirring often. Do not drain.

2. Stir the soup, milk and tuna in the skillet. Top with the cheese. Stir the bread crumbs and butter in a small bowl. Sprinkle over the tuna mixture. Cook until the cheese is melted.

Skillet Mac & Beef

MAKES 6 SERVINGS ■ **PREP TIME:** 5 MINUTES ■ **COOK TIME:** 20 MINUTES

- ¾ pound ground beef (85% lean)
- 1 small onion, chopped (about ¼ cup)
- ½ teaspoon Italian seasoning *or* dried oregano leaves, crushed
- 1 can (10¾ ounces) Campbell's® Condensed Tomato Soup (Regular *or* Healthy Request®)
- ¼ cup water
- 1 cup frozen whole kernel corn
- 3 cups corkscrew-shaped pasta (rotini), cooked without salt and drained
- ¼ cup grated Parmesan cheese

1. Cook the beef, onion and Italian seasoning in a 10-inch skillet over medium-high heat until the beef is well browned, stirring often to separate the meat. Pour off any fat.

2. Stir the soup, water and corn in the skillet and heat to a boil. Reduce the heat to low. Cover and cook for 5 minutes or until the corn is tender. Stir in the pasta and cook until the mixture is hot and bubbling. Sprinkle with the cheese.

Campbell's Fun Food for Kids

Souper Sloppy Joes

MAKES 6 SERVINGS ■ **PREP TIME:** 5 MINUTES ■ **COOK TIME:** 15 MINUTES

1	pound ground beef
1	can (10¾ ounces) Campbell's® Condensed Tomato Soup
¼	cup water
1	tablespoon prepared yellow mustard
6	Pepperidge Farm® Farmhouse Premium White Rolls with Sesame Seeds

1. Cook the beef in a 10-inch skillet over medium-high heat until well browned, stirring often to separate the meat. Pour off any fat.

2. Stir the soup, water and mustard in the skillet and cook until the mixture is hot and bubbling. Spoon the beef mixture on the rolls.

Pizza Fries

MAKES 8 SERVINGS ■ **PREP TIME:** 20 MINUTES ■ **BAKE TIME:** 5 MINUTES

- 1   bag (2 pounds) frozen french fries
- 1   cup Prego® Traditional *or* any variety Prego® Italian Sauce
- 1½ cups shredded mozzarella cheese (about 6 ounces)
-     Diced pepperoni (optional)

1. Prepare the fries according to the package directions. Remove them from the oven. Pour the Italian sauce over the fries.

2. Top with the cheese and pepperoni, if desired.

3. Bake for 5 minutes or until the cheese is melted.

Cheeseburger Pasta

MAKES 5 SERVINGS ■ **PREP TIME:** 5 MINUTES ■ **COOK TIME:** 20 MINUTES

- 1 **pound ground beef**
- 1 **can (10¾ ounces) Campbell's® Condensed Cheddar Cheese Soup**
- 1 **can (10¾ ounces) Campbell's® Condensed Tomato Soup (Regular *or* Healthy Request®)**
- 1½ **cups water**
- 2 **cups *uncooked* medium shell-shaped pasta**

1. Cook the beef in a 10-inch skillet over medium-high heat until well browned, stirring often to separate the meat. Pour off any fat.

2. Stir the soups, water and pasta in the skillet and heat to a boil. Reduce the heat to medium. Cook for 10 minutes or until the pasta is tender, stirring often.

Campbell's Fun Food for Kids

Chocolate Goldfish® Pretzel Clusters

MAKES 24 SERVINGS ■ **PREP TIME:** 5 MINUTES ■ **COOK TIME:** 1 MINUTE
CHILL TIME: 30 MINUTES

1	package (12 ounces) semi-sweet chocolate pieces (about 2 cups)
2½	cups Pepperidge Farm® Pretzel Goldfish® Crackers
1	container (4 ounces) multi-colored nonpareils

1. Line a baking sheet with wax paper.

2. Place the chocolate into a microwavable bowl. Microwave on MEDIUM for 30 seconds. Stir. Repeat until the chocolate is melted and smooth. Add the Goldfish® crackers and stir to coat.

3. Drop the chocolate mixture by tablespoonfuls onto the baking sheet. Sprinkle the clusters with the nonpareils.

4. Refrigerate for 30 minutes or until the clusters are firm. Keep refrigerated until ready to serve.

KITCHEN tip *To wrap for gift-giving, arrange the clusters in a small box lined with colored plastic wrap.*

Campbell's Fun Food for Kids

Chicken Mozzarella

MAKES 4 SERVINGS ■ **PREP TIME:** 5 MINUTES ■ **BAKE TIME:** 20 MINUTES
STAND TIME: 5 MINUTES

- 4 skinless, boneless chicken breasts halves (about 1 pound)
- 1 can (10¾ ounces) Campbell's® Healthy Request® Condensed Tomato Soup
- ½ teaspoon dried Italian seasoning *or* dried oregano leaves
- ½ teaspoon garlic powder
- ¼ cup shredded mozzarella cheese
- 3 cups corkscrew-shaped pasta (rotini), cooked without salt and drained

1. Place the chicken into a 2-quart shallow baking dish. Stir the soup, Italian seasoning and garlic powder in a small bowl. Spoon the soup mixture over the chicken.

2. Bake at 400°F. for 20 minutes or until the chicken is cooked through. Sprinkle with the cheese. Let stand for 5 minutes. Serve the chicken and sauce with the pasta.

Campbell's Fun Food for Kids

Banana-Stuffed French Toast

MAKES 2 SERVINGS ▪ **PREP TIME:** 10 MINUTES ▪ **STAND TIME:** 5 MINUTES
COOK TIME: 15 MINUTES

- ½ cup cholesterol-free egg substitute
- ½ cup nonfat milk
- ¼ teaspoon vanilla extract
- 4 slices Pepperidge Farm® Whole Grain 100% Whole Wheat Bread
  Vegetable cooking spray
- 1 medium banana, sliced
  Cinnamon-sugar*
- 1 cup fresh blueberries
- ½ cup maple-flavored syrup

*For the cinnamon-sugar, stir **1 tablespoon** sugar and ½ **tablespoon** cinnamon in a small bowl.*

1. Beat the egg substitute, milk and vanilla extract in a 2-quart shallow baking dish with a fork or whisk. Add the bread slices and turn to coat. Let stand for 5 minutes.

2. Spray a 12-inch skillet with the cooking spray and heat over medium heat for 1 minute. Add the bread slices and cook until they're lightly browned on both sides.

3. Place **1** toast onto a plate. Top with **half** the banana and another toast. Sprinkle with the cinnamon-sugar and ½ **cup** blueberries. Repeat with the remaining ingredients. Serve with the syrup.

Campbell's Fun Food for Kids

Easy Meatball Parm Heroes

MAKES 4 SANDWICHES ■ **PREP TIME:** 5 MINUTES ■ **COOK TIME:** 25 MINUTES

  2   cups Prego® Traditional Italian Sauce
 16   frozen fully-cooked meatballs (1 ounce *each*)
  4   long hard rolls, split
  1   cup shredded mozzarella cheese (4 ounces)
      Grated Parmesan cheese

1. Heat the Italian sauce and meatballs in a 3-quart saucepan over medium-high heat to a boil. Reduce the heat to low. Cook for 20 minutes or until the meatballs are heated through, stirring occasionally.

2. Divide the meatballs and sauce among the rolls. Sprinkle with the mozzarella and Parmesan cheeses.

Campbells Fun Food for Kids

2-Step Cheesy Pasta Twists

MAKES 4 SERVINGS ■ **PREP TIME:** 20 MINUTES ■ **COOK TIME:** 10 MINUTES

    6   cups corkscrew-shaped pasta (rotini), cooked and drained
    1   jar (24 ounces) Prego® Traditional Italian Sauce *or* Italian Sausage
        & Garlic Italian Sauce
    1   cup shredded mozzarella cheese (about 4 ounces)
    ½   cup Pepperidge Farm® Zesty Italian Croutons, crushed

1. Stir the pasta and Italian sauce in a 10-inch skillet and heat over medium heat until the mixture is hot and bubbling.

2. Reduce the heat to low. Top with cheese and crushed croutons. Cover and cook until the cheese is melted.

Campbell's Fun Food for Kids

Crispy Mozzarella Sticks

MAKES 12 SERVINGS ▪ **THAW TIME:** 40 MINUTES ▪ **PREP TIME:** 20 MINUTES
BAKE TIME: 15 MINUTES ▪ **COOL TIME:** 10 MINUTES

1	egg
1	tablespoon water
¼	cup grated Parmesan cheese
1	package (17.3 ounces) Pepperidge Farm® Puff Pastry Sheets, thawed
1	package (12 ounces) mozzarella cheese snack sticks (12 sticks)
1	cup Prego® Marinara Italian Sauce

1. Heat the oven to 400°F. Beat the egg and water in a small bowl with a fork or whisk. Place the Parmesan cheese into a shallow dish.

2. Unfold **1** pastry sheet on a lightly floured surface. Cut the pastry sheet into **6** (5×3-inch) rectangles. Repeat with the remaining pastry sheet, making **12** in all.

3. Place **1** cheese stick on a long edge of **each** pastry rectangle. Roll up the pastry around the cheese and press the seams and pinch the ends to seal. Brush the tops of the rolls with the egg mixture. Dip the tops into the Parmesan cheese. Place the rolls, seam-side down, onto a baking sheet. Prick the tops of the rolls with a fork.

4. Bake for 15 minutes or until the sticks are golden brown. Remove the sticks from the baking sheet and let cool on a wire rack for 10 minutes.

5. Heat the Italian sauce in a 1-quart saucepan over medium heat until hot and bubbling, stirring occasionally. Serve the sauce with the sticks for dipping.

Cheesy Chicken Pizza

MAKES 4 SERVINGS ▪ **PREP TIME:** 15 MINUTES ▪ **BAKE TIME:** 15 MINUTES

1	package (about 13 ounces) refrigerated pizza dough
½	cup Pace® Picante Sauce
½	cup Prego® Traditional Italian Sauce *or* Roasted Garlic & Herb Italian Sauce
1	cup chopped cooked chicken *or* turkey
½	cup sliced pitted ripe olives
2	green onions, sliced (about ¼ cup)
4	ounces shredded mozzarella cheese (about 1 cup)

1. Heat the oven to 425°F.

2. Unroll the dough onto a greased 12-inch pizza pan. Press the dough into a 12-inch circle. Pinch up the edge to form a rim.

3. Stir the picante sauce and Italian sauce in a small bowl. Spread the picante sauce mixture over the crust to the rim. Top with the chicken, olives, onions and cheese.

4. Bake for 15 minutes or until the cheese is melted and the crust is golden brown.

KITCHEN tip

For a crispier crust, prepare the dough as directed above in step 2. Bake the dough for 5 minutes. Remove the dough from the oven and proceed as directed above in steps 3 and 4.

Campbell's Fun Food for Kids

Easy Chicken & Cheese Enchiladas

MAKES 6 SERVINGS ▪ **PREP TIME:** 15 MINUTES ▪ **BAKE TIME:** 40 MINUTES

- 1 can (10¾ ounces) Campbell's® Condensed Cream of Chicken Soup (Regular *or* 98% Fat Free)
- ½ cup sour cream
- 1 cup Pace® Picante Sauce
- 2 teaspoons chili powder
- 2 cups chopped cooked chicken
- ½ cup shredded Monterey Jack cheese
- 6 flour tortillas (6-inch), warmed
- 1 small tomato, chopped (about ½ cup)
- 1 green onion, sliced (about 2 tablespoons)

1. Heat the oven to 350°F. Stir the soup, sour cream, picante sauce and chili powder in a medium bowl.

2. Stir **1 cup** soup mixture, chicken and cheese in a large bowl.

3. Divide the chicken mixture among the tortillas. Roll up the tortillas and place seam-side up in a 2-quart shallow baking dish. Pour the remaining soup mixture over the filled tortillas. Cover the baking dish.

4. Bake for 40 minutes or until the enchiladas are hot and bubbling. Top with the tomato and onion.

KITCHEN

Stir ½ cup canned black beans, drained and rinsed, into the chicken mixture before filling the tortillas.

  Fun Food for Kids

Tater Tot Casserole

MAKES 5 SERVINGS ▓ **PREP TIME:** 10 MINUTES ▓ **BAKE TIME:** 25 MINUTES

- 1 **pound ground beef**
- 1 **medium onion, chopped (about ½ cup)**
- 1 **can (10¾ ounces) Campbell's® Condensed Cream of Mushroom Soup (Regular *or* 98% Fat Free)**
- 1 **tablespoon ketchup**
- 1 **tablespoon Worcestershire sauce**
- 3 **cups frozen fried potato nuggets**

1. Cook the beef and onion in a 10-inch skillet over medium-high heat until the beef is well browned, stirring to separate the meat. Pour off any fat.

2. Stir the soup, ketchup and Worcestershire in the skillet. Spoon the beef mixture into a 2-quart shallow baking dish. Arrange the potatoes around the inside edge of the baking dish.

3. Bake at 425°F. for 25 minutes or until the potatoes are golden brown.

Campbell's Fun Food for Kids

Sloppy Joe Casserole

MAKES 5 SERVINGS ▪ **PREP TIME:** 15 MINUTES ▪ **BAKE TIME:** 15 MINUTES

- 1 **pound ground beef**
- 1 **can (10¾ ounces) Campbell's® Condensed Tomato Soup (Regular *or* Healthy Request®)**
- ¼ **cup water**
- 1 **teaspoon Worcestershire sauce**
- ⅛ **teaspoon ground black pepper**
- 1 **package (7.5 ounces) refrigerated biscuits (10 biscuits)**
- ½ **cup shredded Cheddar cheese**

1. Heat the oven to 400°F.

2. Cook the beef in a 10-inch skillet over medium-high heat until it's well browned, stirring often to separate the meat. Pour off any fat.

3. Stir the soup, water, Worcestershire and black pepper in the skillet and heat to a boil. Spoon the beef mixture into a 1½-quart casserole. Arrange the biscuits around the inside edge of the casserole.

4. Bake for 15 minutes or until the biscuits are golden brown. Sprinkle the cheese over the beef mixture.

KITCHEN

*Sharp **or** mild Cheddar cheese will work in this recipe.*

Pizza Fondue

MAKES 3 CUPS ▪ **PREP TIME:** 10 MINUTES ▪ **COOK TIME:** 10 MINUTES

- ½   cup finely chopped pepperoni
- 1   small green *or* red pepper, chopped (about ½ cup)
- ½   of an 8-ounce package cream cheese, cut into cubes
- ⅓   cup grated Parmesan cheese
- 1½   cups Prego® Traditional *or* Tomato Basil & Garlic Italian Sauce
  Italian bread cubes *or* tortilla chips

1. Cook the pepperoni and green pepper in a 2-quart saucepan over medium heat for 4 minutes or until the green pepper is tender.

2. Stir in the cream cheese and Parmesan cheese. Cook and stir until the cheese is melted. Stir in the Italian sauce and cook until the mixture is heated through. Serve with the bread cubes for dipping.

Broccoli & Cheese Casserole

MAKES 6 SERVINGS ▪ **PREP TIME:** 10 MINUTES ▪ **BAKE TIME:** 30 MINUTES

1   can (10¾ ounces) Campbell's® Condensed Cream of Mushroom Soup (Regular *or* 98% Fat Free)

½   cup milk

2   teaspoons yellow mustard

1   bag (16 ounces) frozen broccoli flowerets, thawed

1   cup shredded Cheddar cheese (4 ounces)

⅓   cup dry bread crumbs

2   teaspoons butter, melted

1. Stir the soup, milk, mustard, broccoli and cheese in a 1½-quart casserole.

2. Stir the bread crumbs and butter in a small bowl. Sprinkle the crumb mixture over the broccoli mixture.

3. Bake at 350°F. for 30 minutes or until the mixture is hot and bubbling.

Rice Is Nice: Add **2 cups** cooked white rice to the broccoli mixture before baking.

Cheese Change-Up: Substitute mozzarella cheese for the Cheddar.

Hearty Lasagna Soup

MAKES 4 SERVINGS ■ **PREP TIME:** 10 MINUTES ■ **COOK TIME:** 25 MINUTES

- 1 **pound ground beef**
- 1 **small onion, chopped (about ¼ cup)**
- 1 **teaspoon minced garlic**
- ¼ **teaspoon dried parsley flakes**
- 3½ **cups Swanson® Beef Broth (Regular, 50% Less Sodium *or* Certified Organic)**
- 1 **can (14.5 ounces) diced tomatoes**
- ¼ **teaspoon Italian seasoning, crushed**
- 1½ **cups *uncooked* mafalda *or* corkscrew-shaped pasta (rotini)**
- ¼ **cup grated Parmesan cheese**

1. Cook the beef, onion, garlic and parsley in a 3-quart saucepan over medium-high heat for 10 minutes, or until it's well browned, stirring often to separate the meat. Pour off any fat.

2. Stir the broth, tomatoes and Italian seasoning in the saucepan and heat to a boil.

3. Stir the pasta in the saucepan. Reduce the heat to medium and cook for 10 minutes or until the pasta is tender. Stir in the cheese. Serve with additional cheese, if desired.

Campbell's Fun Food for Kids

Banana Blast Smoothie

MAKES 2 SERVINGS ▪ **PREP TIME:** 5 MINUTES

1   cup Diet V8 Splash® Juice Drink, any flavor

½   cup plain nonfat yogurt

1   medium banana, sliced

2   ice cubes

Put all of the ingredients in a blender. Cover and blend until they're smooth.

Cool & Creamy Fruit Smoothies

MAKES 2 SERVINGS ▪ **PREP TIME:** 10 MINUTES

1 cup V8 Splash® Smoothies Strawberry Banana

½ cup peach sorbet *or* your favorite flavor

½ cup vanilla low-fat yogurt

½ cup fresh strawberries, cut into quarters

Put all of the ingredients in a blender. Cover and blend until they're smooth. Serve immediately.

Inside Out Pizza Casserole

MAKES 6 SERVINGS ▪ **PREP TIME:** 20 MINUTES ▪ **BAKE TIME:** 30 MINUTES
STAND TIME: 10 MINUTES

½	of a 15-ounce package refrigerated pie crust (1 crust)
1	tablespoon vegetable oil
1	pound bulk pork sausage
1	package (8 ounces) sliced mushrooms
1	large onion, chopped (about 1 cup)
1½	cups Prego® Traditional *or* Roasted Garlic & Herb Italian Sauce
4	ounces sliced pepperoni, coarsely chopped
2	cups shredded mozzarella cheese (about 8 ounces)
½	cup grated Parmesan cheese

1. Heat the oven to 400°F. Let the pie crust stand at room temperature for 15 minutes or until it's easy to handle.

2. Heat the oil in a 10-inch skillet over medium-high heat. Add the sausage and cook until it's well browned, stirring frequently to separate the meat. Pour off any fat.

KITCHEN

Crimping the edges of the crust helps the crust adhere to the edges of the casserole, making it less likely to shrink.

3. Add the mushrooms and onion and cook until they're tender. Stir in the Italian sauce and pepperoni and cook until the mixture is hot and bubbling. Remove the skillet from the heat and let cool slightly. Stir in the mozzarella and Parmesan cheeses. Spoon the mixture into a 2-quart casserole.

4. Place the crust over the sausage mixture and crimp the edges. Cut several slits in the crust.

5. Bake for 30 minutes or until the crust is golden. Let the casserole stand for 10 minutes before serving.

Fun Food for Kids

Easy Chicken Mozzarella Sandwich

MAKES 1 SERVING ▪ **PREP TIME:** 5 MINUTES ▪ **COOK TIME:** 10 MINUTES

- ⅓ cup Prego® Traditional *or* Roasted Garlic & Herb Italian Sauce
- 1 refrigerated, fully cooked breaded chicken cutlet (about 3½ ounces)
- 1 slice mozzarella cheese (about 1 ounce)
- 2 slices Italian bread

1. Place the Italian sauce and chicken in a 6-inch skillet over medium heat. Cover and cook until heated through.

2. Top the chicken with the cheese. Cover and cook until the cheese is melted. Place the chicken on **1** bread slice. Top with sauce and remaining bread slice.

Campbell's Fun Food for Kids

Easy Italian Burger Melt

MAKES 6 SERVINGS ▪ **PREP TIME:** 10 MINUTES ▪ **BAKE TIME:** 20 MINUTES

1½ **pounds ground beef**

1 **can (10¾ ounces) Campbell's® Condensed Tomato Soup**

⅓ **cup water**

1 **teaspoon dried oregano leaves, crushed**

1 **cup shredded mozzarella cheese (about 4 ounces)**

1. Heat the oven to 400°F.

2. Shape the ground beef into **6** patties, ½-inch thick **each**. Place them in a 2-quart shallow baking dish.

3. Stir the soup, water and oregano in a small bowl until the mixture is smooth. Pour over the patties. Top with the cheese.

4. Bake for 20 minutes or until the patties are cooked through. Serve the patties on rolls or hamburger buns.

Holiday & Party Time

Green Bean Casserole
(recipe page 200)

Green Bean Casserole

MAKES 12 SERVINGS ■ **PREP TIME:** 10 MINUTES ■ **BAKE TIME:** 30 MINUTES

2 cans (10¾ ounces *each*) Campbell's® Condensed Cream of Mushroom Soup (Regular *or* 98% Fat Free)

1 cup milk

2 teaspoons soy sauce

¼ teaspoon ground black pepper

8 cups cooked cut green beans

2⅔ cups French's® French Fried Onions

1. Stir the soup, milk, soy sauce, black pepper, beans and **1⅓ cups** onions in a 3-quart casserole.

2. Bake at 350°F. for 25 minutes or until the bean mixture is hot and bubbling. Stir the bean mixture. Sprinkle with the remaining onions.

3. Bake for 5 minutes or until the onions are golden brown.

To add crunch: Add ½ **cup** sliced almonds to the onion topping.

For bacon lovers: Add **4** slices bacon, cooked and crumbled, to the bean mixture.

KITCHEN

Use **2 bags** (16 to 20 ounces *each*) frozen green beans, **4 packages** (9 ounces *each*) frozen green beans, **4 cans** (about 16 ounces *each*) green beans **or** about **3 pounds** fresh green beans for this recipe.

To add a festive touch: Add ½ **cup** chopped red pepper with the soup.

For cheese lovers: Stir in **1 cup** shredded Cheddar cheese with the soup. Omit the soy sauce. Sprinkle with an additional ½ **cup** Cheddar cheese when adding the remaining onions.

Crowd-Pleasing Vegetable Casserole

MAKES 12 SERVINGS ▪ **PREP TIME:** 10 MINUTES ▪ **BAKE TIME:** 25 MINUTES

1	can (26 ounces) Campbell's® Condensed Cream of Mushroom Soup (Regular *or* 98% Fat Free)
1½	cups shredded Swiss cheese (about 6 ounces)
⅔	cup sour cream
¼	teaspoon ground black pepper
2	bags (16 ounces *each*) frozen vegetable combination (broccoli, cauliflower, carrots), cooked and drained
2	cans (2.8 ounces *each*) French's® French Fried Onions (2⅔ cups)

1. Stir the soup, **1 cup** cheese, sour cream, black pepper, vegetables and **1 can** onions in a 3-quart shallow baking dish.

2. Bake at 400°F. for 20 minutes or until the vegetable mixture is hot and bubbling. Stir the vegetable mixture. Sprinkle with the remaining cheese and onions.

3. Bake for 5 minutes or until the onions are golden brown.

Herb Roasted Turkey with Pan Gravy

MAKES 12 SERVINGS ▪ **PREP TIME:** 15 MINUTES ▪ **COOK TIME:** 3 HOURS
STAND TIME: 10 MINUTES

1¾ cups Swanson® Chicken Stock
3 tablespoons lemon juice
1 teaspoon dried basil leaves, crushed
1 teaspoon dried thyme leaves, crushed
⅛ teaspoon ground black pepper
1 (12- to 14-pound) turkey
¼ cup all-purpose flour

1. Stir the stock, lemon juice, basil, thyme and black pepper in a small bowl.

2. Roast the turkey according to the package directions, basting occasionally with the stock mixture during cooking. Let the turkey stand for 10 minutes before slicing.

3. Remove the turkey from the roasting pan. Spoon off any fat.

4. Stir the remaining stock mixture and flour in a small bowl until the mixture is smooth. Add the stock mixture to the roasting pan. Cook and stir over medium heat until the mixture boils and thickens. Serve the turkey with the gravy.

Campbell's Holiday & Party Time

Stuffed Pork Tenderloins en Croûte

MAKES 8 SERVINGS ▪ **THAW TIME:** 40 MINUTES ▪ **PREP TIME:** 20 MINUTES
BAKE TIME: 30 MINUTES ▪ **COOL TIME:** 10 MINUTES

1	egg
1	tablespoon water
1	tablespoon vegetable oil
1	large onion, chopped (about 1 cup)
1	bag (7 ounces) dried mixed fruit, coarsely chopped (about 1½ cups)
¼	cup port wine
2	(1 pound *each*) pork tenderloins
⅓	cup all-purpose flour
½	of a 17.3-ounce package Pepperidge Farm® Puff Pastry Sheets (1 sheet), thawed

1. Heat the oven to 375°F. Beat the egg and water in a small bowl with a fork or whisk.

2. Heat the oil in a 10-inch skillet over medium heat. Add the onion and cook until tender. Stir the fruit and wine in the skillet. Cook for 5 minutes or until all the liquid is evaporated. Remove the skillet from the heat. Let cool to room temperature.

3. Coat the pork with the flour.

4. Unfold the pastry sheet on a lightly floured surface. Roll the pastry sheet into a 14-inch square. Cut into **2** (14×7-inch) rectangles. Spread **half** the onion mixture lengthwise down the center of each rectangle. Top **each** with **1** pork tenderloin. Brush the edges of the pastry with the egg mixture. Fold the pastry over the pork and press to seal. Place the wrapped pork seam-side down onto a baking sheet. Tuck the ends under to seal. Brush the pastry with the egg mixture.

5. Bake for 30 minutes or until the pastries are golden brown. Remove the pastries from the baking sheet and let cool on wire racks for 10 minutes.

Holiday Cookie House

MAKES 1 COOKIE HOUSE ■ **PREP TIME:** 2 HOURS ■ **STAND TIME:** 3 HOURS

3   egg whites
½   teaspoon cream of tartar
1   box (16 ounces) confectioners' sugar
     Assorted Pepperidge Farm® Cookies and Crackers

1. Cut a 15×15-inch square from heavy cardboard or thick foam core board for the base. Cut the walls and roof of the house from heavy cardboard.

2. Beat the egg whites, cream of tartar and confectioners' sugar in a large bowl with an electric mixer on high speed for 5 minutes or until stiff peaks form. Spoon **about 1 cup** icing into a pastry bag. Cover the bowl with a damp cloth to prevent the remaining icing from drying out.

3. Assemble the house using the icing as the "glue." Make sure to "glue" the walls to the base as well as to each other, holding each piece in place for 5 minutes before moving on to the next. Let stand for 3 hours or until the house is completely dry before decorating.

4. Decorate the house with the Pepperidge Farm® cookies and crackers, using the icing as the "glue." Spread the icing on the base to make snow.

KITCHEN tip

Here's a fun project that the kids will love. Get creative by using cookies to cover a cardboard farmhouse . . . it makes a wonderful centerpiece for the holidays.

Hazelnut Cappuccino Rugalach

MAKES 64 PIECES ■ **THAW TIME:** 40 MINUTES ■ **PREP TIME:** 20 MINUTES
BAKE TIME: 15 MINUTES ■ **COOL TIME:** 30 MINUTES

1	package (17.3 ounces) Pepperidge Farm® Puff Pastry Sheets (2 sheets)
¾	cup sugar
2	tablespoons cappuccino coffee drink mix
1	teaspoon ground cinnamon
⅔	cup hazelnuts, toasted and finely chopped
4	ounces milk chocolate, chopped

1. Thaw the pastry sheets at room temperature for 40 minutes or until they're easy to handle. Heat the oven to 375°F. Lightly grease or line 2 baking sheets with parchment paper.

2. Stir the sugar, coffee mix and cinnamon in a small bowl. Sprinkle ¼ **cup** sugar mixture onto a work surface. Unfold **1** pastry sheet onto the sugar mixture. Sprinkle with ¼ **cup** sugar mixture. Roll the pastry sheet into a 12×10-inch rectangle. Sprinkle with ⅓ **cup** nuts. Gently press the nuts into the pastry with a rolling pin. Cut the pastry into **4** (12×2½-inch) strips. Cut **each** strip into **4** (3-inch) pieces. Cut **each** piece diagonally in half into **2** triangles, making **32** triangles. Starting at the wide side, roll the triangles up to make a crescent shape. Place the pastries pointed-side down on a baking sheet. Repeat with the remaining pastry sheet, sugar mixture and nuts.

3. Bake for 15 minutes or until the pastries are golden. Remove the pastries from the baking sheets and cool on wire racks.

4. Place the chocolate into a microwavable bowl. Microwave on HIGH for about 30 seconds. Stir until the chocolate is melted and smooth. Drizzle the chocolate over the cookies. Cookies can be stored in an airtight container for up to 1 week.

KITCHEN tip

Cookies can be prepared through step 3 above, then frozen for up to 3 months. Reheat in a 300°F. oven for about 5 minutes or until the cookies are crisp. Let cool on a wire rack and drizzle with the melted chocolate just before serving.

Quick and Easy Chocolate Fondue

MAKES 12 SERVINGS ■ **PREP TIME:** 5 MINUTES ■ **COOK TIME:** 5 MINUTES

2 cups semi-sweet chocolate pieces

½ cup (1 stick) butter

Suggested Dippers: Pepperidge Farm® Cinnamon Swirl Bread, toasted and cut into strips; Pepperidge Farm® Chessmen® Cookies; Pepperidge Farm® Gingerman Homestyle Cookies; or Pepperidge Farm® Milano® Cookies

1. Cook and stir the chocolate and butter in an 8-inch heavy skillet over low heat for 5 minutes or until the chocolate is melted and smooth.

2. Pour the chocolate mixture into a fondue pot or a decorative bowl. Serve warm with the *Suggested Dippers*.

KITCHEN tip

*You can also use this chocolate mixture to make festive chocolate and candy-coated puff pastry strips: Thaw **1** sheet Pepperidge Farm® Puff Pastry. Unfold the pastry sheet on a lightly floured surface and roll into a 12-inch square. Cut into **72** (4×½-inch) strips and place onto baking sheets. Bake at 400°F. for 20 minutes or until golden brown. Dip the pastry strips in the warm chocolate mixture and sprinkle with crushed candy canes. Place on wax paper-lined baking sheets. Refrigerate or let stand at room temperature until chocolate is set.*

Chicken Dijon in Pastry Shells

MAKES 6 SERVINGS ▪ **PREP TIME:** 35 MINUTES ▪ **COOK TIME:** 30 MINUTES

- 2 tablespoons butter
- 4 skinless, boneless chicken breast halves (about 1 pound), cut into strips
- 1½ cups broccoli flowerets
- 1½ cups sliced mushrooms (about 4 ounces)
- 1 can (10¾ ounces) Campbell's® Condensed Cream of Chicken Soup (Regular *or* 98% Fat Free)
- ¼ cup milk
- 2 tablespoons Dijon-style mustard
- 1 package (10 ounces) Pepperidge Farm® Puff Pastry Shells, prepared according to package directions

1. Heat **1 tablespoon** butter in a 10-inch skillet over medium-high heat. Add the chicken and cook until well browned and cooked through, stirring often. Remove the chicken from the skillet.

2. Heat the remaining butter in the skillet over medium heat. Add the broccoli and mushrooms and cook until the vegetables are tender, stirring occasionally.

3. Stir the soup, milk and mustard in the skillet and heat to a boil. Return the chicken to the skillet and cook until the mixture is hot and bubbling. Spoon the chicken mixture into the pastry shells.

Heavenly Sweet Potatoes

MAKES 8 SERVINGS ▪ **PREP TIME:** 10 MINUTES ▪ **BAKE TIME:** 20 MINUTES

Vegetable cooking spray

1   can (40 ounces) cut sweet potatoes in heavy syrup, drained

¼   teaspoon ground cinnamon

⅛   teaspoon ground ginger

¾   cup Swanson® Chicken Broth (Regular, Natural Goodness® *or* Certified Organic)

2   cups miniature marshmallows

1. Heat the oven to 350°F.

2. Spray a 1½-quart casserole with cooking spray.

3. Put the potatoes, cinnamon and ginger in an electric mixer bowl. Beat at medium speed until almost smooth. Add the broth and beat until potatoes are fluffy. Spoon the potato mixture in the prepared dish. Top with the marshmallows.

4. Bake for 20 minutes or until heated through and marshmallows are golden brown.

Holiday Banana Bread Pudding

MAKES 6 SERVINGS ▪ **PREP TIME:** 15 MINUTES ▪ **BAKE TIME:** 25 MINUTES

- 8 slices Pepperidge Farm® Cinnamon Swirl Bread, cut into cubes (about 5 cups)
- 2 large bananas, cut into ¼-inch-thick slices
- ¾ cup semi-sweet chocolate pieces
- 1½ cups heavy cream
- 3 eggs
- ¼ cup packed brown sugar
- 2 teaspoons vanilla extract

1. Heat the oven to 350°F. Lightly grease a 1½-quart baking dish.

2. Place the bread cubes, bananas and chocolate pieces into the baking dish. Beat the heavy cream, eggs, brown sugar and vanilla extract in a medium bowl with a fork or whisk. Pour the cream mixture over the bread mixture. Stir and press the bread mixture into the cream mixture to coat.

3. Bake for 25 minutes or until a knife inserted in the center comes out clean.

Apple Pecan Pastries

MAKES 6 SERVINGS ▪ **THAW TIME:** 40 MINUTES ▪ **PREP TIME:** 20 MINUTES
BAKE TIME: 15 MINUTES ▪ **COOL TIME:** 10 MINUTES

- ½ of a 17.3-ounce package Pepperidge Farm® Puff Pastry Sheets (1 sheet)
- 1 cup packed brown sugar
- ½ cup all-purpose flour
- 1 teaspoon ground cinnamon
- ⅛ teaspoon ground nutmeg
- 2 cups peeled, diced Granny Smith apples
- 1 cup chopped pecans
- 1 tablespoon cold butter, cut into pieces
- Confectioners' sugar

1. Thaw the pastry sheet at room temperature for 40 minutes or until it's easy to handle. Heat the oven to 375°F. Lightly grease a baking sheet.

2. Stir the brown sugar, flour, cinnamon and nutmeg in a medium bowl. Add the apples, pecans and butter and toss to coat.

3. Unfold the pastry sheet on a lightly floured surface. Roll the pastry sheet into a 15×10-inch rectangle. Brush the pastry sheet with water. With the long side facing you, spoon the apple mixture on the pastry to within 2 inches of the long sides and to the edge of the short sides. Starting at a long side, roll up like a jelly roll. Cut the pastry roll into **12** (1¼-inch) slices. Place the slices 2 inches apart on the baking sheet.

4. Bake for 15 minutes or until the pastries are golden. Remove the pastries from the baking sheet and cool on a wire rack. Sprinkle with the confectioners' sugar.

KITCHEN tip

You can substitute chopped walnuts for the pecans if you like.

Double-Apricot Glazed Ham

MAKES 32 SERVINGS ▪ **PREP TIME:** 15 MINUTES ▪ **BAKE TIME:** 2 HOURS

- 1 cup dried apricots
- 1 cup Swanson® Chicken Stock
- ½ cup packed brown sugar
- 1 fully-cooked whole boneless ham* (6 to 8 pounds)
- 2 tablespoons butter
- ½ cup finely chopped shallots
- 2 jars (12 ounces *each*) apricot preserves
- ¼ cup Dijon-style mustard
- 2 teaspoons grated orange zest

You can use a 3-pound fully-cooked half boneless ham for 16 servings. Prepare as directed above, but reduce the remaining ingredients in half and the cooking time to 1 hour or until the ham is heated through.

1. Place the apricots and stock into a microwave-safe measuring cup. Microwave on HIGH for 2 minutes. Let the mixture cool. Remove the apricots and cut into strips. Reserve the stock. Stir the apricots, sugar and ¼ **cup** reserved stock in a small bowl.

2. Place the ham into a roasting pan. Bake at 325°F. for 2 hours or until the ham is heated through. Brush with the apricot mixture during the last 30 minutes of baking and baste frequently with the pan drippings.

3. Heat the butter in a 10-inch skillet over medium heat. Add the shallots and cook until they're tender. Stir in the preserves, mustard, orange zest and remaining reserved stock and heat to a boil. Reduce the heat to low. Cook and stir for 10 minutes or until the stock mixture is slightly thickened.

4. Slice the ham and serve with the apricot sauce.

  Holiday & Party Time

Crab Appetizer Napoleons

MAKES 12 SERVINGS ■ **THAW TIME:** 40 MINUTES ■ **PREP TIME:** 20 MINUTES
BAKE TIME: 10 MINUTES ■ **COOL TIME:** 10 MINUTES

½ of a 17.3-ounce package Pepperidge Farm® Puff Pastry Sheets
(1 sheet), thawed

1 package (8 ounces) cream cheese, softened

1 tablespoon milk

1 tablespoon prepared horseradish

¼ teaspoon ground black pepper

1 can (about 6 ounces) refrigerated pasteurized crabmeat, drained

4 green onions, sliced (about ½ cup)

½ cup sliced almonds

Paprika

1. Heat the oven to 400°F.

2. Unfold the pastry sheet on a lightly floured surface. Cut the pastry
sheet into **12** (2-inch) circles with a cutter. Place the pastry circles onto
a baking sheet.

3. Bake for 10 minutes or until the pastries are golden brown. Remove
the pastries from the baking sheet and let cool on a wire rack for
10 minutes. Split **each** pastry into **2** layers, making **24** in all.

4. Stir the cream cheese in a medium bowl until smooth. Stir in the milk,
horseradish, black pepper and crabmeat.

5. Spread the crabmeat mixture on
12 bottom pastry layers. Top with
the onions, almonds and top pastry
layers. Sprinkle with the paprika.

 KITCHEN tip *To soften the cream cheese, remove from the wrapper and place onto a microwave-safe plate; microwave on HIGH 15 seconds.*

Easy Party Meatballs

MAKES 8 SERVINGS ▪ **PREP TIME:** 5 MINUTES ▪ **COOK TIME:** 6 HOURS

3	cups (1 pound 10 ounces) Prego® Marinara Italian Sauce
1	jar (12 ounces) grape jelly
½	cup prepared chili sauce
2½	pounds frozen fully-cooked meatballs, cocktail size

1. Stir the Italian sauce, jelly, chili sauce and meatballs in a 4½-quart slow cooker.

2. Cover and cook on LOW for 6 to 7 hours* or until the meatballs are cooked through. Serve the meatballs on a serving plate with toothpicks.

Or on HIGH for 3 to 4 hours.

KITCHEN tip

*Larger-size **or** turkey meatballs can also be used, if desired.*

For a special touch, serve with cranberry chutney for dipping.

Loaded Baked Potato Casserole

MAKES 8 SERVINGS ▪ **PREP TIME:** 15 MINUTES ▪ **BAKE TIME:** 35 MINUTES

- 1 bag (32 ounces) Southern-style hash-brown potatoes, thawed (about 7½ cups)
- 1 can (6 ounces) French's® French Fried Onions (2⅔ cups)
- 1 cup frozen peas, thawed
- 1 cup shredded Cheddar cheese (4 ounces)
- 4 slices bacon, cooked and crumbled
- 2 cans (10¾ ounces *each*) Campbell's® Condensed Cream of Celery Soup (Regular *or* 98% Fat Free)
- 1 cup milk

1. Stir the potatoes, **1⅓ cups** of the onions, peas, cheese and bacon in a 13×9-inch (3-quart) shallow baking dish. Stir the soup and milk in a medium bowl. Pour the soup mixture over the potato mixture. **Cover**.

2. Bake at 350°F. for 30 minutes or until hot. Stir.

3. Sprinkle with the remaining onions. Bake for 5 minutes more or until the onions are golden brown.

KITCHEN tip

To thaw the hash browns, cut off 1 corner on bag and microwave on HIGH for 5 minutes.

Campbell's Holiday & Party Time

Beef Wellington

MAKES 10 SERVINGS ▪ **THAW TIME:** 40 MINUTES ▪ **PREP TIME:** 45 MINUTES
CHILL TIME: 1 HOUR ▪ **BAKE TIME:** 25 MINUTES

1	beef tenderloin (2 to 2½ pounds)
	Ground black pepper (optional)
1	egg
1	tablespoon water
1	tablespoon butter
2	cups finely chopped mushrooms
1	medium onion, finely chopped (about ½ cup)
½	of a 17.3-ounce package Pepperidge Farm® Puff Pastry Sheets (1 sheet), thawed

1. Heat the oven to 425°F. Place the beef into a lightly greased roasting pan. Season with the black pepper, if desired. Roast for 30 minutes or until a meat thermometer reads 130°F. Cover the pan and refrigerate for 1 hour.

2. Reheat the oven to 425°F. Beat the egg and water in a small bowl with a fork or whisk.

3. Heat the butter in a 10-inch skillet over medium-high heat. Add the mushrooms and onion and cook until the mushrooms are tender and all the liquid is evaporated, stirring often.

4. Unfold the pastry sheet on a lightly floured surface. Roll the pastry sheet into a rectangle 4 inches longer and 6 inches wider than the beef. Brush the pastry sheet with the egg mixture. Spoon the mushroom mixture onto the pastry sheet to within 1 inch of the edges. Place the beef in the center of the mushroom mixture. Fold the pastry over the beef and press to seal. Place seam-side down onto a baking sheet. Tuck the ends under to seal. Brush the pastry with the egg mixture.

5. Bake for 25 minutes or until the pastry is golden brown and a meat thermometer reads 140°F.

Spinach-Cheese Swirls

MAKES 20 PIECES ▪ **THAW TIME:** 40 MINUTES ▪ **PREP TIME:** 20 MINUTES
BAKE TIME: 15 MINUTES ▪ **COOL TIME:** 10 MINUTES

1	egg
1	tablespoon water
½	cup shredded Muenster cheese *or* Monterey Jack cheese
¼	cup grated Parmesan cheese
1	green onion, chopped (about 2 tablespoons)
⅛	teaspoon garlic powder
½	of a 17.3-ounce package Pepperidge Farm® Puff Pastry Sheets (1 sheet), thawed
1	package (about 10 ounces) frozen chopped spinach, thawed and well drained

KITCHEN tip

Make sure to remove as much liquid as you can from the spinach before adding it to the pastry. If it's too wet, it may make the pastry soggy.

1. Heat the oven to 400°F. Beat the egg and water in a small bowl with a fork or whisk.

2. Stir the Muenster cheese, Parmesan cheese, onion and garlic powder in a medium bowl.

3. Unfold the pastry sheet on a lightly floured surface. Brush the pastry sheet with the egg mixture. Top with the cheese mixture and spinach. Starting with a short side, roll up like a jelly roll. Cut into **20** (½-inch) slices. Place the slices, cut-side down, onto baking sheets. Brush the slices with the egg mixture.

4. Bake for 15 minutes or until the pastries are golden brown. Remove the pastries from the baking sheets and let cool on wire racks for 10 minutes.

Herbed Chicken in Pastry

MAKES 4 SERVINGS ▪ **THAW TIME:** 40 MINUTES ▪ **PREP TIME:** 35 MINUTES
CHILL TIME: 15 MINUTES ▪ **BAKE TIME:** 25 MINUTES ▪ **COOL TIME:** 10 MINUTES

1	egg
1	tablespoon water
4	skinless, boneless chicken breast halves (about 1 pound)
	Ground black pepper (optional)
2	tablespoons butter
½	of a 17.3-ounce package Pepperidge Farm® Puff Pastry Sheets (1 sheet), thawed
1	container (4 ounces) garlic & herb spreadable cheese
¼	cup chopped fresh parsley

1. Heat the oven to 400°F. Beat the egg and water in a small bowl with a fork or whisk.

2. Season the chicken with the black pepper, if desired. Heat the butter in a 10-inch skillet over medium-high heat. Add the chicken and cook for 10 minutes or until it's well browned on both sides. Remove the chicken to a plate. Cover the plate and refrigerate for 15 minutes or up to 24 hours.

3. Unfold the pastry sheet on a lightly floured surface. Roll the pastry sheet into a 14-inch square. Cut into **4** (7-inch) squares.

4. Spread **about 2 tablespoons** cheese spread in the center of **each** pastry square. Top **each** with **1 tablespoon** parsley and **1** chicken breast. Brush the edges of the pastry squares with the egg mixture. Fold the corners of the pastry squares to the center over the chicken and press to seal. Place the filled pastries seam-side down onto a baking sheet. Brush the pastries with the egg mixture.

5. Bake for 25 minutes or until the pastries are golden brown. Let the pastries cool on the baking sheet for 10 minutes.

Spiced Pot Roast

MAKES 8 SERVINGS ▪ **PREP TIME:** 5 MINUTES ▪ **MARINATE TIME:** 12 HOURS
BAKE TIME: 3 HOURS ▪ **STAND TIME:** 10 MINUTES

- 3 tablespoons packed brown sugar
- 2 teaspoons ground cloves
- 2 teaspoons ground allspice
- 2 teaspoons ground cinnamon
- 1 teaspoon cracked black pepper
- 1 (4-pound) boneless beef bottom round roast *or* beef chuck pot roast
- 2 cups Swanson® Beef Stock
- 1 bottle (12 ounces) stout *or* dark beer
  Hot boiled potatoes
  Chopped fresh parsley (optional)

1. Stir the brown sugar, cloves, allspice, cinnamon and black pepper in a large bowl. Add the beef and turn to coat. Cover the bowl and refrigerate for 12 hours or overnight.

2. Place the beef in a 6-quart oven-safe saucepot. Pour the stock and beer over the beef. Cover the saucepot.

3. Bake at 350°F. for 3 hours or until the beef is fork-tender. Remove the beef from the saucepot and let stand for 10 minutes. Thinly slice the beef. Serve with the stock mixture and the potatoes. Sprinkle with the parsley, if desired.

Campbell's Holiday & Party Time

Hearty Sausage, Peppers & Potatoes

MAKES 8 SERVINGS ■ **PREP TIME:** 20 MINUTES ■ **BAKE TIME:** 30 MINUTES

- 2 pounds sweet *or* hot Italian pork sausages, cut into 2-inch pieces
- 6 red new potatoes, cut into quarters
- 2 medium green peppers, cut into 2-inch-long strips (about 3 cups)
- 1 package (8 ounces) sliced mushrooms
- ½ of a large sweet onion, sliced (about ½ cup)
- 2 cups Prego® Traditional *or* Tomato, Basil & Garlic Italian Sauce

1. Stir the sausage, potatoes, peppers, mushrooms and onion in a 13×9×2-inch baking dish. Add the Italian sauce and stir to coat.

2. Bake at 400°F. for 30 minutes or until the sausage is cooked through and the vegetables are tender.

KITCHEN tip

For a heartier meal, serve the sausage mixture on long sandwich rolls.

Sausage-Stuffed Green Peppers

MAKES 8 SERVINGS ▓ **PREP TIME:** 20 MINUTES ▓ **BAKE TIME:** 40 MINUTES

- 1 tablespoon vegetable oil
- 1 pound sweet Italian pork sausage, casing removed
- 1 medium onion, chopped (about ½ cup)
- 1 teaspoon dried oregano leaves, crushed
- 1 cup shredded part-skim mozzarella cheese (about 4 ounces)
- 4 medium green peppers, seeded and cut in half lengthwise
- 2 cups Prego® Traditional Italian Sauce *or* Tomato, Basil & Garlic Italian Sauce

1. Heat the oven to 400°F. Heat the oil in a 10-inch skillet over medium-high heat. Add the sausage and cook until it's well browned, stirring often to separate the meat. Add the onion and oregano and cook until the onion is tender. Pour off any fat. Stir in the cheese.

2. Arrange the peppers in a 3-quart shallow baking dish. Spoon the sausage mixture into the peppers. Pour the Italian sauce over the filled peppers. Cover the baking dish.

3. Bake for 40 minutes or until the peppers are tender.

Campbell's

Holiday Brie en Croûte

MAKES 12 SERVINGS ▪ **THAW TIME:** 40 MINUTES ▪ **PREP TIME:** 15 MINUTES
BAKE TIME: 20 MINUTES ▪ **STAND TIME:** 45 MINUTES

- 1   egg
- 1   tablespoon water
- ½   of a 17.3-ounce package Pepperidge Farm® Puff Pastry Sheets (1 sheet), thawed
- ½   cup apricot preserves *or* seedless raspberry jam
- ⅓   cup dried cranberries
- ¼   cup toasted sliced almonds
- 1   (13- to 16-ounce) Brie cheese round
- 1   package (13 ounces) Pepperidge Farm® Entertaining Quartet Distinctive Crackers

1. Heat the oven to 400°F. Beat the egg and water in a small bowl with a fork.

2. Unfold the pastry sheet on a lightly floured surface. Roll the pastry sheet into a 14-inch square. Spread the preserves on the pastry to within 2 inches of the edge. Sprinkle with the cranberries and almonds. Place the cheese in the center of the pastry. Fold the pastry up over the cheese to cover. Trim the excess pastry and press to seal. Brush the seam with the egg mixture. Place seam-side down onto a baking sheet. Decorate with the pastry scraps, if desired. Brush with the egg mixture.

3. Bake for 20 minutes or until the pastry is golden brown. Let stand for 45 minutes. Serve with the crackers.

Pastry Twists

MAKES 28 TWISTS ▪ **THAW TIME:** 40 MINUTES ▪ **PREP TIME:** 20 MINUTES
BAKE TIME: 10 MINUTES ▪ **COOL TIME:** 10 MINUTES

1   **egg**

1   **tablespoon water**

½   **of a 17.3-ounce package Pepperidge Farm® Puff Pastry Sheets
     (1 sheet), thawed**

Assorted Fillings

1. Heat the oven to 400°F. Beat the egg and water in a small bowl with a fork. Lightly grease a baking sheet.

2. Sprinkle the work surface with the flour. Unfold the pastry on the work surface. Roll the pastry into a 14×10-inch rectangle. Cut the rectangle in half lengthwise. Brush the halves with the egg mixture. Top **1** half with *Filling*. Place the remaining half over the filling, egg-side down. Roll gently with a rolling pin to seal.

3. Cut the pastry crosswise into **28** (½-inch) strips. Twist the strips and place them 2 inches apart on the baking sheet, pressing down the ends. Brush the pastries with the egg mixture.

4. Bake for 10 minutes or until the pastries are golden brown. Let the pastries cool on the baking sheet on a wire rack for 10 minutes.

Assorted Fillings:

Parmesan Cheese: Stir ¼ **cup** grated Parmesan cheese, **1 tablespoon** chopped fresh parsley and ½ **teaspoon** dried oregano leaves, crushed, in a small bowl.

Choco-Berry: Spread the pastry half with **2 tablespoons** seedless raspberry jam and sprinkle with ⅓ **cup** mini semi-sweet chocolate pieces.

Cinnamon-Sugar: Stir **2 tablespoons** sugar and **1 teaspoon** ground cinnamon in a small bowl.

Maple-Glazed Ham

MAKES 12 SERVINGS ■ **PREP TIME:** 15 MINUTES ■ **BAKE TIME:** 2 HOURS

¼ cup pure maple syrup

2 tablespoons Dijon-style mustard

6- to 9-pound fully-cooked bone-in spiral ham

2 teaspoons cornstarch

1¾ cups Swanson® Chicken Stock

¼ teaspoon dried thyme leaves, crushed

⅛ teaspoon freshly ground black pepper

1 tablespoon butter

¼ cup chopped shallots

1. Stir **2 tablespoons** syrup and **1 tablespoon** mustard in a small bowl.

2. Place the ham into a roasting pan and cover loosely with foil. Bake at 325°F. for 1 hour 30 minutes.

3. Brush the ham with the syrup mixture and bake, uncovered, for 30 minutes or until the ham is heated through, brushing occasionally with the syrup mixture.

4. Stir the cornstarch, stock, thyme, black pepper, remaining syrup and remaining mustard in a small bowl until the mixture is smooth.

5. Heat the butter in a 1-quart saucepan over medium heat. Add the shallots and cook until they're tender. Stir the cornstarch mixture in the skillet. Cook and stir until the mixture boils and thickens. Serve with the ham.

Chocolate Pirouette®-Crusted Cake

MAKES 8 SERVINGS ■ **THAW TIME:** 90 MINUTES ■ **PREP TIME:** 1 MINUTES

- 1 box (19.6 ounces) Pepperidge Farm® Chocolate Fudge 3 Layer Cake
- ½ of a 13.5-ounce canister Pepperidge Farm® Pirouette® Chocolate Hazelnut Rolled Wafers (about 18)

1. Thaw the cake according to the package directions. Place the cake onto a serving dish.

2. Cut the wafers into 2½-inch-long pieces. Place the wafers upright, side-by-side, all around the edge of the cake, pressing them gently into the frosting. Place any remaining wafers on top of the cake.

KITCHEN tip

This cake can be prepared up to 2 days ahead and stored in the refrigerator.

Campbell's Holiday & Party Time

Italian Marinated Chicken

MAKES 6 SERVINGS ■ **PREP TIME:** 5 MINUTES ■ **MARINATE TIME:** 30 MINUTES
GRILL TIME: 15 MINUTES

1¾	cups Swanson® Chicken Stock
1	tablespoon canned diced tomatoes, drained
1	teaspoon grated Parmesan cheese
½	teaspoon Italian seasoning, crushed
¼	teaspoon garlic powder
6	skinless, boneless chicken breasts halves (about 1½ pounds)

1. Stir the stock, tomatoes, cheese, Italian seasoning and garlic powder in a shallow nonmetallic dish or a resealable plastic bag. Add the chicken and turn to coat. Cover the dish or seal the bag and refrigerate for 30 minutes.

2. Lightly oil the grill rack and heat the grill to medium. Remove the chicken from the stock mixture.

3. Grill the chicken for 15 minutes or until it's cooked through, turning it over once halfway through cooking and brushing often with the stock mixture. Discard the remaining stock mixture.

Harvest Fruit Stuffing

MAKES 8 SERVINGS ■ **PREP TIME:** 10 MINUTES ■ **COOK TIME:** 10 MINUTES
BAKE TIME: 20 MINUTES

1¾ cups Swanson® Chicken Broth (Regular, Natural Goodness® *or* Certified Organic)

¼ cup apple juice

1 cup cut-up mixed dried fruit

1 stalk celery, sliced (about ½ cup)

1 medium onion, chopped (about ½ cup)

5 cups Pepperidge Farm® Herb Seasoned Stuffing

1. Heat the oven to 350°F.

2. Stir the broth, apple juice, dried fruit, celery and onion in a 3-quart saucepan. Heat to a boil over medium-high heat. Reduce the heat to low. Cover and cook for 5 minutes or until the vegetables are tender. Remove the saucepan from the heat. Add the stuffing and stir lightly to coat.

3. Spoon the stuffing into a 1½-quart casserole. Bake for 20 minutes or until it's hot.

Lemon Herb Broccoli Casserole

MAKES 6 SERVINGS ▪ **PREP TIME:** 10 MINUTES ▪ **BAKE TIME:** 30 MINUTES

- 1 can (10¾ ounces) Campbell's® Condensed Cream of Chicken with Herbs Soup
- ½ cup milk
- 1 tablespoon lemon juice
- 4 cups frozen broccoli cuts, thawed
- 1 can (2.8 ounces) French's® French Fried Onions (1⅓ cups)

1. Stir the soup, milk, lemon juice, broccoli and ⅔ **cup** onions in a 1½-quart casserole. Cover the casserole.

2. Bake at 350°F. for 25 minutes or until the broccoli is tender. Stir the broccoli mixture. Sprinkle with the remaining onions.

3. Bake, uncovered, for 5 minutes or until the onions are golden brown.

KITCHEN tip *To thaw the broccoli, microwave on HIGH for 3 minutes.*

Roasted Chicken with Stuffing & Gravy

MAKES 6 SERVINGS ■ **PREP TIME:** 30 MINUTES
COOK TIME: 3 HOURS ■ **STAND TIME:** 10 MINUTES

- ¼ cup (½ stick) butter
- 1 stalk celery, sliced (about ½ cup)
- 1 medium onion, chopped (about ½ cup)
- 1¼ cups water
- 1 medium carrot, shredded (about ½ cup) (optional)
- 4 cups Pepperidge Farm® Herb Seasoned Stuffing
- 1 roasting chicken (5 to 7 pounds)
  Vegetable oil
- 1 jar (12 ounces) Campbell's® Slow Roast Chicken Gravy

1. Heat the butter in a 3-quart saucepan over medium heat. Add the celery and onion and cook until they're tender. Stir in the water and carrot. Remove the saucepan from the heat. Add the stuffing and mix lightly.

2. Remove the package of the giblets and neck from the chicken cavity. Rinse the chicken with cold water and pat dry with a paper towel. Spoon the stuffing lightly into the neck and body cavities. Fold the loose skin over the stuffing. Tie the ends of the drumsticks together.

3. Place the chicken, breast-side up, on a rack in a shallow roasting pan. Brush the chicken with the oil. Insert a meat thermometer into the thickest part of the meat, not touching the bone.

4. Roast for 2½ to 3 hours or until the drumstick moves easily and the center of the stuffing reaches 165°F., basting occasionally with the pan drippings. Let the chicken stand for 10 minutes before slicing.

5. Heat the gravy in a 1-quart saucepan over medium-high heat until it's hot and bubbling. Serve the gravy with the chicken.

KITCHEN tip *Bake any remaining stuffing in a covered casserole with the chicken for 30 minutes or until the stuffing is hot.*

Spicy Honey-Mustard Sausage Wraps

MAKES 8 SERVINGS ▪ **THAW TIME:** 40 MINUTES ▪ **PREP TIME:** 20 MINUTES
BAKE TIME: 25 MINUTES ▪ **COOL TIME:** 10 MINUTES

- 1   **egg**
- 1   **tablespoon water**
- ½   **of a 17.3-ounce package Pepperidge Farm® Puff Pastry Sheets (1 sheet), thawed**
- 2   **tablespoons honey mustard**
- 1   **package (16 ounces) turkey *or* beef kielbasa, cut into 8 pieces**

1. Heat the oven to 375°F. Beat the egg and water in a small bowl with a fork or whisk.

2. Unfold the pastry sheet on a lightly floured surface. Roll the pastry sheet into a 13×9-inch rectangle. Brush the pastry with the honey mustard. Cut the pastry into **8** (about 4½×3-inch) rectangles.

3. Place **1** piece kielbasa in the center of **each** pastry rectangle. Brush the edges with the egg mixture. Fold the pastry over the kielbasa and press to seal. Place the filled pastries seam-side down onto a baking sheet. Brush the pastries with the egg mixture.

4. Bake for 25 minutes or until the pastries are golden brown. Remove the pastries from the baking sheets and let cool on a wire rack for 10 minutes. Serve with additional honey mustard for dipping.

KITCHEN

Recipe may be doubled.

 Holiday & Party Time